Thrive

Cynthia A Smith

Tapestry of Beauty Ministries

Acknowledgements

This study would not be possible without those the Lord placed in my life to encourage me along the way.

- My husband Sean. He has always believed in me. He is my biggest cheerleader and fan. I am so thankful for him.
- My daughters, Robin & Ellie-thank you for your encouragement and understanding when I needed to concentrate. Thank you, Robin, for proofreading for me and helping me grow as a writer.
- Kristin Vanderlip-thank you for birthing the idea of thriving in the desert! You spoke this into my life at just the right time!
- Sara Turnquist-thank you friend for always being willing to listen to my ideas and thoughts. Thank you for encouraging me to actually put down words. You told me that you can always edit garbage (which you doubted I would write) but you can't edit nothing!
- Sophia & Matthew Tucker-thank you for encouraging me to follow the leading of the Holy Spirit! Your support and friendship mean so much to me! You have given me a space to explore the gifts the Lord has given me.
- The ladies of Tapestry of Beauty Ministries-thank you ladies for proofing this study. Thank you for encouraging me to write and share what the Holy Spirit has laid on my heart.
- Mom Life Ministries-thank you for providing a space where I could spend time with the Lord! I was in a dry place in my walk with the Lord! The friendships and community that Mom Life created helped me to realize a dream of mine to write about the Word of God!

Thrive Second Edition Introduction

The righteous shall flourish like a palm tree,
He shall grow like a cedar in Lebanon.
Those who are planted in the house of the LORD
Shall flourish in the courts of our God.
They shall still bear fruit in old age;
They shall be fresh and flourishing,
To declare that the LORD is upright;
He is my rock, and there is no
unrighteousness in Him.
Psalm 92:12-15

Welcome to Thrive the Second Edition. This has been such an amazing journey for me over the last year. I have learned so much. The first edition of Thrive was such a labor of love and I am thankful that so many have learned about the fruit of the Spirit. Having never written a Bible study before I did not really know what I was doing, and the Holy Spirit was faithful to speak. This second edition comes from more revelation from the Lord!

The Lord gave me the word Thrive for the year 2020. The year has changed, and I have a new word, but the Lord still wants to see us thrive, to grow, to flourish in our walk with Him. He still desires to see the women of God walk in fullness and to step into their calling. And we all have a calling. We all can thrive where we are, and we can do it today.

To thrive is to grow, expand, to flourish, and to advance in any valuable thing. Isn't that what we all long to see in our lives? How do we walk this out with the Lord? What is our part in this process? What is the Lord's part? How do we know what thriving looks like? What does the Lord see as thriving? That is what we will be looking at in this study.

This passage from Psalm 92 is a good place to see what it looks like to be a woman who thrives. When we are planted in the house of the Lord, we thrive, we flourish, we grow. It is about having a relationship with the Lord. We thrive when we are in His presence daily. It is about walking daily with the Spirit. Where it speaks of being planted in His courts represents us always being in His presence. It is about wanting to know Him in a very personal and real way. We thrive, flourish, and grow when we let the roots of our lives grow down into His foundation. We grow strong with our root firmly established in Him. He feeds us with His life-giving waters. We can be strong in Him throughout all of our lives.

There are things that we will need to do in this process of learning what it looks like to thrive in the Lord. It is simple and yet often we miss it. His Spirit is what causes us to thrive, in order to do that… we must spend time renewing our minds. Romans 12:2 tells us "to not be conformed to this world" and we are going to need to look at the things in our lives that are keeping us stuck and floundering. We thrive when we are transformed through the renewing of our minds. As we are renewing our minds, we are taking thoughts that keep us from growing and letting the Holy Spirit change them. We spend time soaking in the truth of God's Word and the Spirit works in our hearts, minds, bodies, soul, and spirit to transform us, to help us thrive.

Please join me on this journey as we look at the fruit of the Spirit. This time through I want us to really see how the fruit is the character of the Holy Spirit. It is who He is, and He wants to overwhelm us with the fruit. Starting here is what will help us to experience and express the fruit. We cannot thrive through effort on our part. We thrive when the Spirit extends the fruit to us, and we pass it along to others!

So as my dear friend Susan Dixson says, "Together we go!"

Section One

Holy Spirit

The Fruit of the Spirit

But the fruit of the Spirit is love, joy, peace,
patience, kindness, goodness, faithfulness,
gentleness, and self-control.
Galatians 5:22

What do you think about when you hear someone talk about the fruit of the Spirit? Do you think that here is another list of things that you must "do"? Do you write this off as some unattainable list that is for someone, anyone, just not you? Or do you think of this fruit as the character of the Living God as expressed in the Holy Spirit?

This passage is one that we see all over the place. We can go on Pinterest and see beautiful image after beautiful image. Many of our homes have one of these beautiful images hanging on our walls. If you are anything like me, we look at these beautifully printed words and think, "Wow! I wish I could be these things. I would be happy just being one of these." They can become a chain that keeps us doubting ourselves and feeling defeated.

This study is called Thrive because that is what the Lord wants from His daughters. He wants us to thrive, and He gives us the Holy Spirit to be our source. Thinking about a plant thriving, we are the plant, and the Holy Spirit pours Himself, His character, His fruit into each one as we walk by His Spirit. We will look at what that means in a later lesson.

Let's start with a quick look at who is the Holy Spirit? He is a part of the Trinity: God the Father, God the Son (Jesus), and God the Holy Spirit. They are equal. There is not one part of the Trinity that has more authority or power than the other. This has been an area that I have had to renew my mind about. The church I grew up in did not talk a lot about the Spirit. His job was to convict us of our sins and that was pretty much it. The truth is that the Holy Spirit is fully God, He is all knowing, all powerful, and in all places at all times.

Thankfully I have learned that the Holy Spirit is so much more. He is a gift that the Father sends to us to help us walk out the process of becoming more like Christ. The Holy Spirit was sent to us when Jesus was taken up into heaven after His resurrection. Here is Jesus telling us what the Holy Spirit will do.

But the Helper (Comforter, Advocate, Intercessor—Counselor, Strengthener, Standby), the Holy Spirit, whom the Father will send in My name [in My place, to represent Me and act on My behalf], He will teach you all things. And He will help you remember everything that I have told you. John 14:26

The Lord did not want to leave us alone. He wants us to know where we should go. So, the Holy Spirit was sent at Pentecost to dwell in believers so they could know the good, perfect, and pleasing will of God. (Romans 12:2)

We need to take a quick overview of the story of the Bible. Please know that this is highly simplified. We read in Genesis that God created all that is: the animals, plants, man, everything! He created man differently than the rest of creation though. He created man in His image, male and female. He created us and loved us and wanted to have a relationship with us. Sin got in the way though. Adam and Eve decided to disobey the command of God and ate the forbidden fruit.

God in His goodness did not want to stay detached from man, so He created the law and sacrifices for us to be Holy as He is holy. Guess what? We still could not obey Him. The Old Testament shows how mankind tried to follow Him, to walk in His ways, but failed time and time again. So, God created a way that once and for all would allow us to have a relationship with Him. He sent His Son Jesus to follow the law perfectly. We are told that Jesus was fully human yet did not sin!

For we do not have a High Priest who is unable to sympathize and understand our weaknesses and temptations, but One who has been tempted [knowing exactly how it

feels to be human] in every respect as we are, yet without [committing any] sin.
Hebrews 4:15

Jesus lived here on earth, was tempted to follow after His own will but chose to obey His Father. He then became the ultimate perfect sacrifice. He willingly went to the Cross and died so that we could be free from sin and be in God's presence forever! Jesus then was raised to new life having defeated sin and death. Jesus proved once and for all that He was God's Son and that He is the way to life everlasting! Amen!

But God was not finished there! No! Jesus told His disciples that He had to go away so that another could come to help us. We see what happened in the Old Testament when mankind tried to be holy in their own strength. It all went horribly wrong. This time the Holy Spirit would come, and He would enable us to obey. He would enable us to be molded in the image of Jesus!

The fruit of the Holy Spirit is the character of the Spirit. He is love, He is joy, He is peace. He is all of these things. We often talk about the fruit as separate pieces, but the Greek here makes it clear that fruit is singular. These are also the characteristics of the rest of the Trinity. God the Father has these same characteristics. Jesus has them. Through the Holy Spirit we have this fruit and can walk in them.

Admit it, there is something about you that you do not like. There is something you want to change and see victory over. The Lord can show us an area He wants us to surrender to Him in order that He can fill the emptiness and fix all the broken pieces. Instead of turning to Him and letting Him fill and fix us, we strive. We work hard to change, to be better, and get no results. Sweet friend, we are not meant to fix ourselves. We cannot fill up what is missing. Only the Holy Spirit can fix us and fill us and cause us to thrive.

Are you ready to learn about who the Holy Spirit is? Through this study we will learn about Him. Learn how He expresses the fruit and how His indwelling power changes you, fills you, fixes you. He wants to be the source behind us, spurring us on to being conformed into His likeness.

Here are some questions to help you understand the Holy Spirit better!

What is your experience with the Holy Spirit? What have you been taught about Him? How has this shaped how you think about the fruit of the Spirit?

Look at John 16:13. What does it say about whose authority the Holy Spirit speaks from? Whose words does He repeat? God's

John 14:15-17 speaks about hearing the Holy Spirit's voice. Who hears His voice? Are you able to hear His voice? Christian's

Faith Activation: Do a Think on Model about Holy Spirit. There is a worksheet provided for you.

Thrive and the Abundance of Holy Spirit

The thief does not come except to steal,
and to kill, and to destroy. I have come
that they may have life, and that they may
have it more abundantly.
John 10:10

Thrive is such a powerful word. It is a hopeful word. The Lord wants to develop this in our lives. Jesus came so that we will have eternal life but that was not all. He came so that we may have a relationship with God right this minute. We can walk with Him today and have His fruit develop in us. He is blessing us with so much more than just eternal salvation. He wants us to walk in His abundance today.

Let us look at some definitions to help us understand what we have in Christ Jesus. The Greek word for abundance means exceeding some number or measure or rank or need; over and above, more than is necessary, super-added. It would be enough to have salvation from our sins, but we have been given over and above.

For us to get a picture of what it is to thrive in the abundance of Jesus Christ, let us look at some Scriptures from the Word. What do you see in these passages?

Luke 6:38 *Holy Spirit will give us a good life if we seek him*

Ephesians 3:20 *Able to do more than we as k or imagine, according to his power at work in us.*

1 Timothy 1:14 *grace poured on me*

God gives us so much.

In the world today it is hard to feel like we are thriving. There have been some hard and heavy things that have happened. We have had a pandemic, racial injustice, and severe weather. It would be easy to believe that this abundant life has been put on hold. We have just come out of a season of isolation due to a pandemic, worldwide we have had political strife, and racial injustice. This may make it hard for you to feel like you can thrive. In the early church they were able to thrive in the face of persecution and political tyranny. We can have the Lord's abundance right this minute.

What is going on in your life right now? Are you having a hard time seeing God's abundance? Spend time praying that the Holy Spirit will open your eyes to the abundance He is giving you right this minute.

We need to be aware of what the thief does to try to take away that abundance. He comes to steal and to kill and to destroy. He wants to steal our joy, kill our faith, and destroy our testimony. My Mom has lived with us until recently and watching her decline mentally and physically is so hard. I must confess that there are times when I lose patience and fuss at her. There are times I get angry and vent to someone. Sadness over all that is happening can threaten to overtake me. The thief wants me to believe that I am all alone and that this is just too much for me to handle. He wants me to try and solve my own problems and make myself happy. He is wanting me to live a life of defeat and imprisonment.

The feelings of being overwhelmed and lonely are the schemes of the thief as he is trying to steal, kill, and destroy. He wants us to try to draw from our own strength. Even in times of ease he is trying to get us to believe we have to trust in ourselves. This is opposite of what the Spirit gives. When we turn to the Holy Spirit daily, we see a deep well of love, joy, peace, patience, kindness, goodness, faithfulness, gentleness, and self-control. Walking with the Spirit gives us that well to draw from and thrive!

Here are some questions to help you understand the Holy Spirit better!

What does it look like to you to thrive? *Keep my food Boundaries*

How is your vision of thriving the same or different from what we see in the

Word of God?

Faith Activation: Write out Scripture prayers asking the Lord for the ability to line up our vision of thriving with His. A description of how to write a Scripture prayer is provided in the Appendix.

I will not worship any other God for the Lord, whose name is jealous is a jealous God

The Fullness of Christ

*For the entire fullness of God's nature dwells
bodily in Christ, and you have been filled
by Him, who is the head over
every ruler and authority.*
Colossians 2:9-10

The message of this verse is very powerful. We have the fullness of God dwelling in us. The Greek word for fullness means to fill to the top: so that nothing shall be wanting to full measure or fill to the brim. There is nothing lacking for those of us who are in Christ Jesus.

Jesus told us in John 14 that He had to go to the Father so that the Holy Spirit would come. The Spirit has come to remind us of the things that Jesus taught, to be our Counselor, to remain with us and in us, and to be the Spirit of truth. This is different from the Old Testament where the Holy Spirit came to people for a specific time with a specific job. We have the Holy Spirit with us always and therefore we have the fullness of God.

Here are some verses about what we have through the Holy Spirit. What do they say we have through the Holy Spirit?

Ephesians 1:13-14 *everything God has planned for us, a praising & glorious life*

1 Corinthians 3:16 *God is present in me*

1 Corinthians 2:11-13 *gifts of life & salvation*

1 Corinthians 2:15-16 *We have Christ's spirit*

These truths are important as we go forward in this study. The fruit of the Spirit is love, joy, peace, patience, kindness, goodness, faithfulness, gentleness, and self-control. These originate from God, and they represent His character.

His character dwells in the Holy Spirit and in Christ Jesus they dwell in us. These amazing gifts often overwhelm me with their goodness.

We live in a world that encourages us to be better people. There are so many books and programs that promote self-improvement. They are not of real value because the effort is all on the self.

We must be the ones making changes and developing new habits. This self-striving will not work for us. To see true transformation in our lives we must do as Romans 12:2 says, "Do not be conformed to this age, but be transformed by the renewing of your mind, so that you may discern what is the good, and acceptable and perfect will of God." We become a new person, someone completely different than who we were before. How does this happen? Through renewing the mind. Renewed is a renovation, or complete change for the better. This renewal changes how our minds think and process information for the better. Isn't that what we look for in the pages of all the self-help books? We need to renew our minds to the fact that we have all we need for life and godliness (2 Peter 1:3) through the Holy Spirit.

Throughout this study I will be encouraging you to renew your minds daily. We will be looking at the Holy Spirit, the different aspects of the fruit, who we are in Christ, and how to thrive. It will be important that we let the Holy Spirit change how we think about all of this. There will be activities each day called Faith Actions. These tools are here to help you actively renew your mind. I would encourage you to do these Faith Actions several times a day. Some are quick and can be done over and over. There are a couple of tools that you may need to work on throughout the day. The point of these activities is to focus on what is true about the Word of God and what it says about you. So, hang on and prepare to be transformed and thrive!

Here are some questions to help you understand the Holy Spirit better!

What does it mean to be filled with the fullness of God?

The Holy Spirit dwells in us.

Faith Activation: Prepare to start this process of transformation by simply being quiet with the Lord. You may want to journal about what transformation you desire to see as you go through this study. Ask the Lord to reveal to you what He wants you to learn and write it down.

Walk in the Spirit

I say then: Walk in the Spirit, and you
shall not fulfill the lust of the flesh.
Galatians 5:16

Doesn't this sound easy? Walk in the Spirit and you will thrive. The truth is that oftentimes it is difficult and leads to frustration. But guess what? It is not meant to be a difficult practice for us, my sisters. Walking in the Spirit leads to life, and we are going to spend some time really looking at what it looks like to walk in the Spirit.

Let's start with a little exercise. I want you to close your eyes and think of taking a walk with someone very special to you. It could be a friend, a spouse, or a grandparent. You are walking and talking and fellowshipping. You are telling them of all the cares you carry. There is no detail too big or too small that you do not share. You ask for wisdom. You laugh. You cry. You just enjoy being in their presence.

This is what the Spirit desires from us. He wants us to walk with Him daily. He wants us to share our joys, fears, hurts, sicknesses, and our love. This is not an exhaustive list, it is just that the Spirit wants us walking with Him, talking to Him, and learning of Him. The Holy Spirit has many things He wants to share with us. Let's look at a few of them.

First, He wants to teach us about the things that Jesus taught His disciples. Jesus, Himself, tells the disciples why He must go in John 14:26. "But the Helper, the Holy Spirit, whom the Father will send in My name, He will teach you all things, and bring to your remembrance all things that I said to you." Jesus could not be with His disciples all the time. Jesus knew that soon the leaders of the Jews would have Him killed and the disciples would need a Helper. Jesus knew that we would need a helper.

Second, through the Holy Spirit we have been given the fullness of God. In

Colossians we see that it pleased God that His fullness should be in Jesus and through the Holy Spirit, this fullness resides in each and every believer. This can be hard to comprehend. When we came to salvation, God, and all that He is, came to dwell in each one of us. If we are the bearers of God's fullness, then there is nothing lacking in us. We have all that we need for life and godliness (2 Peter 1:3). We do not need to add anything to the finished work of the Cross. The Holy Spirit reminds us that we are complete. This is a notion that is lacking in today's culture. We think we must do something or be something else to be complete. Knowing the truth of our completeness through the Holy Spirit brings us freedom and life!

Third, the Holy Spirit shares His gifts with us. There are many places in the New Testament that talk about the gifts of the Spirit. These gifts include prophecy, speaking in tongues, wisdom, hospitality, healing, evangelism, and the ability to distinguish between spirits. This is by no means a complete list, but each one of us has been given a gift or gifts. There are many on-line spiritual gift inventories that you can take to find out your own.

Fourth, when we face trials and temptations, the Holy Spirit is the one who gives us the weapons we need to fight. Let's look at 2 Corinthians 10:3-5:

For though we walk in the flesh, we do not war according to the flesh. For the weapons of our warfare are not carnal but mighty in God for pulling down strongholds, casting down arguments and every high thing that exalts itself against the knowledge of God, bringing every thought into captivity to the obedience of Christ,

In this passage we see that the battle that we face is not fought with worldly weapons. The Holy Spirit is the one whose weapons we use. It is His weapons that are mighty to pull down the strongholds and cast down all arguments. He shares His powers with us to live in victory.

As we think about walking in the Spirit, all these and more-we learn from Him. He shares who He is with us. We find ourselves becoming more and more like Him. Practically, how do we walk in the Spirit? We spend time in the Word. We pray. We worship. We fellowship with other believers. We renew our minds to the truth of the Word. The more time we spend in fellowship with the Holy Spirit, the more like Him we become. The things that we once struggled with become less of a struggle. We find ourselves imitating Him and the things He does. We thrive when we walk in the Spirit.

Here are some questions to help you understand the Holy Spirit better!

Look at Ephesians 1:15-23 and list all the things that we see we receive because of the Holy Spirit. *Spirit of wisdom + Revelation so that we may Better Know him Know the hope to which he has called us. The riches of his glorious inheritance in his holy people. Incomparable great power*

What are some of the gifts you see that the Holy Spirit has given you? *Peace Joy*

What practical steps can you take to walk in the Spirit? There is no right or wrong answer as you are on your own journey with the Lord and your walk will look different from others. *Read the Bible Pray Affiliate with Believers*

Faith Activation: Today ask Holy Spirit to give you a vision of what it looks like for you to walk with Him. Each person has an individual journey with the Lord and your journey looks different than mine. Write down what He shows you. *Eat healthy foods. Avoid sugar.*

The Spirit vs the Flesh

For the flesh desires what is against the Spirit,
and the Spirit desires what is against the flesh;
these are opposed to each other,
so that you don't do what you want.
Galatians 5:17

Today we begin to switch our focus from the Spirit to looking at the works of the flesh. The flesh is such a hard term to define. The Strong's Concordance and Greek dictionary define the flesh as the earthly nature of man apart from God. In a sermon by Andrew Farley, he said that the flesh is man's way of trying to live life. It is us trying to work to transform ourselves into what Christ desires. It is us refusing to give up control of the events that come into our lives.

When uncomfortable feelings well up inside me, it is so tempting to run to things I think will make me feel safe and secure. After fussing at Mom for forgetting what I just told her for the fifth time, it is so tempting to eat something sweet. For years, I have been trying to make the uncomfortable feeling of disappointing someone go away. The things that I have tried have never made the feelings subside.

We desire to feel at peace deep within ourselves. It is also a desire to be accepted and loved. These are good desires. It is ok to desire peace. The King James Version of the Bible does not use the word desire, it uses the word lust. We tend to connect lust with sexual sins, but when we are chasing after something that we feel we must have to be happy, we are in lust. Many of the works of the flesh are not bad in and of themselves. The problem comes when we start lusting after them. It is a problem when we look to these acts as our salvation and not to the Lord. It is an over-desiring of something and leads to death.

The Spirit and flesh desire opposing things. The Spirit desires the things of

God. He desires that the world see the goodness and mercy of God. He desires that we truly understand what our salvation entails. The Spirit works out this desire as He transforms us into women who reflect the glory of God.

The flesh desires the opposite. It seeks to trap us, to make us prisoners of our own desires. It desires its own way and will do whatever it takes to get it. It desires to be fed more and more and more, never being satisfied. The Spirit desires life, and life abundantly, while the flesh desires death.

Walking in the Spirit we learn to desire what the Spirit desires, the things of God. We will desire to see the truth of God reflected in our lives to others. We will desire to be transformed and throw off that which holds us back.

Last year the Holy Spirit called me to stop reading a lot of fiction. I wasted a lot of time reading novels as a way to stop feeling uncomfortable. As I renewed my mind over this, I stopped enjoying the fiction and started desiring more and more of the Word. Our desires will line up with the truth of the Holy Spirit because we will understand where our true identity lies.

Here are some questions to help you understand the Holy Spirit better!

Here are some more verses about the Holy Spirit. Knowing more about who He is will help us know what He desires. What do you see here?

Romans 8:11   He gives us life because his spirit lives in us

Romans 8:26   Spirit intercedes & lets us know what to pray for

2 Corinthians 3:17-18   Transforms us to his image

Faith Activation: Today make Scripture Cards. Place them up around your house and read them often. It will help us understand more about the Holy Spirit. A description of how to write Scripture Cards is provided in the Appendix.

Section Two

Love
&
Faithfulness

The Holy Spirit is Love!

Beloved, let us love one another, for love is of God;
and everyone who loves is born of God
and knows God. He who does not love
does not know God, for God is love.
1 John 4:7-8

Love is a major focus of our society. We all search for it and praise the Lord it is found in God. The passage tells us that God is love that love is of God, and that those who love are born of God. Isn't that wonderful? We all want to love and feel love in return. In God we see this desire come to fruition.

We see God as love throughout the Scriptures. The first time we see God loving mankind is in Deuteronomy 7:7. Here we see God talking to His chosen people, Israel. "The LORD did not set His love on you nor choose you because you were more in number than any other people, for you were the least of all peoples;". We see that God loves Israel but not because of anything they did. He chose to love them, and He chose to love us. We do not have anything that sets up apart to gain His attention. He is love and He chooses to love us.

The Old Testament of the Bible is a story of God as love. In the beginning we see God create everything that is including mankind. He created man in His own image and set them in a garden. He walked with them and talked with them. They sinned and ruined the relationship they had with God. God in His great love covered their nakedness through a sacrifice of animals. We see how He showed man His love in order to rectify this break in relationship.

Throughout the Old Testament we see God continually offers a way to reconcile man back to Himself. He did this because we are His creation, and He loves us. Mankind would often respond in a positive way, following Him and His ways. Quickly, though, they would go back to living how they wanted and forgetting God.

God showered them with His love and would continually try to draw them back into relationship. Finally, He decided to offer His Son to live and be the sacrifice for us. We see this in John 3:16 "For God so loved the world that He gave His only begotten Son, that whoever believes in Him should not perish but have everlasting life." God's love is so big that He did not withhold His own Son. He did it for me and for you! Jesus came to be the righteous sacrifice through His life, death, and resurrection. He met all the laws, or ways for us to have a relationship with God and did it because of love.

I am always in awe of what God did through sending His Son to be the way for me to have reconciliation with God. The fact that He loves me that much is hard to comprehend. It is even more crazy when I think He did that for me even when I did not deserve it. This only goes to speak more about His love. "But God demonstrates His own love toward us, in that while we were still sinners, Christ died for us." Romans 5:8

Jesus is not the last way we see God sharing His love with us. After Jesus was resurrected and returned to heaven, the Holy Spirit was given. The Holy Spirit is an extension of God and His love for us. Through the Holy Spirit we can finally walk in the holiness of God. The Holy Spirit is part of the Godhead and gives us access to all of God's love. This love is what creates in us a desire to surrender and be more like Christ.

Here are some questions to help you understand how the Holy Spirit is love!

What area do you desire to see the Holy Spirit's love?

How have you experienced God's great love in your life?

Faith Activation: Do a Think on Model about love. There is a worksheet provided for you.

What Love Looks Like!

Though I speak with the tongues of men and of angels, but have not love, I have become sounding brass or a clanging cymbal. And though I have the gift of prophecy, and understand all mysteries and all knowledge, and though I have all faith, so that I could remove mountains, but have not love, I am nothing. And though I bestow all my goods to feed the poor, and though give my body to be burned, but have not love, it profits me nothing. Love suffers long and is kind; love does not envy; love does not parade itself, is not puffed up; does not behave rudely, does not seek its own, is not provoked, thinks no evil; does not rejoice in iniquity, but rejoices in the truth; bears all things, believes all things, hopes all things, endures all things. Love never fails. But whether there are prophecies, they will fail; whether there are tongues, they will cease; whether there is knowledge, it will vanish away. For we know in part, and we prophesy in part. But when that which is perfect has come, then that which is in part will be done away. When I was a child, I spoke as a child, I understood as a child, I thought as a child; but when I became a man, I put away childish things. For now, we see in a mirror, dimly, but then face to face. Now I know in part, but then I shall know just as I also am known. And now abide faith, hope, love, these three; but the greatest of these is love.

1 Corinthians 13 (NKJV)

Our world loves love, and we spend so much of our time chasing after it. The thing is the world has a very messed up definition of love. Love without Christ is not true love. When writing this lesson I looked on the Internet to see how people define love. The website Thought Catalog had some pretty interesting answers.[1]

One person said it is giving another person the power to destroy you and trusting them not to. One answer was to have the other person's best interest at heart. Another person likened it to an incurable disease. Several people suggested that we avoid it if at all possible. There were a lot that defined it as

---

[1] 36 Definitions of Love
https://thoughtcatalog.com/marisa-donnelly/2016/04/36-definitions-of-love-according-to-urban-dictionary/#:~:text=1%20Love%20is%20giving%20someone%20the%20power%20to,of%20tricking%20people%20into%20reproducing.%20More%20items...%20

a chemical reaction and feeling. There were a couple of people who said it was unexplainable. Is it any wonder that when the world chases after love, not knowing what it really is, that so many people are not thriving in love?

Before we go on in this study, how do you define love?

Thankfully, we have the Word of God. It is inspired, God breathed, and it is profitable for teaching us the truth of love. Love is found in Christ Jesus. God so loved this world that He sent Jesus Christ, His Son to die for us. He has our best interests at heart. He has such great affection for us that He provided a way for us to have a relationship with us. Paul, in his writings to the church in Corinth, gives us a very detailed definition of love. Paul is really contrasting how the world loves and how Christ loves.

We have a choice when it comes to walking out the love we see expressed here in 1 Corinthians 13. Friend, the Holy Spirit came to dwell in us the moment we gave our lives to Jesus Christ. He came and brought with Him all the fruit of the Spirit and shared it with each one of us. Our choice is whether we will turn towards the world and respond as the world does. On the other hand, we have the option of turning towards the Holy Spirit and drawing from this fruit.

The love of Christ suffers long, is patient, and is kind. This is expressed by being patient with situations, emotions, and people. It is not surprising that when we get uncomfortable we want that discomfort to end. We can be in a situation where we feel frustrated with the behavior of someone else. We can be standing in line waiting for our turn and feel like it is forever. We have a choice: we can turn to the Holy Spirit and let His love help us to respond to situations out of that love. We can be calm and patiently deal with people and situations in love. We can also choose to react in a worldly way. We can snap at those around us. We can complain and speak unkindly to those in the line around us.

Christ's love does not envy. Through the indwelling Spirit we do not envy what others have, or rather we rejoice with them. The world sees what others have and either want it for themselves or does not want the other person to have it either. Envy causes so much strife. Envy comes from a place where we fear we will not be taken care of and that we will lack. We fear this sense of lack and the feelings of inadequacies. The love that comes as a fruit of the Holy Spirit fills every place in our hearts.

We do not fear need or feel inadequate because we know that the Lord has provided us with all that we need. There is nothing that we need that He will not provide because we are assured of His love.

Christ's love does not parade itself, meaning it does not go around asking for people to look and admire, it does not puff up, and it does not behave rudely. Through the Holy Spirit we want to shine the light on those around us. We celebrate their victories. We celebrate Jesus and what He is working out in their lives. The world thinks that it should parade itself around and show off for others to see. I think a lot of us have seen that on social media and can get a clear picture of what this looks like. It is not very pretty. The world also seems to celebrate being rude. I think the thought behind demanding its own way is that no one else will, so I must take care of myself! Is it any wonder that this is not loving? The focus is all on self and not the Lord and definitely not others.

Friends, we are so blessed with all that the Lord has done for us and in us. We can seek out the good for others. It is difficult to be provoked when we are grounded in this love. Christ's love enables us to think the thoughts of the Spirit. We will not think evil. Instead of rejoicing in the iniquity of this world, in Christ we rejoice in the truth. As believers, we rejoice in seeing the things of the Lord come to fruition. There are so many movies, programs, news stories, and social media posts that focus on the evil that exists in this world.

The love of Christ leads to life. It leads to thriving, growing, maturing, and shining. Christ's love is seeking the best in others. It is about giving of oneself. It is about not holding grudges. It is about patiently loving those who seem unlovable. We know this love because He first loved us.

The love that the world offers leads to death. It leads to self-centered lives. The world does not know what real love is and we see the devastating results. The world has so messed up the truth about what love is that it cannot be defined. The love the world offers has led to envies, strife, hatred, brokenness, and sadness. Watching the news is painful because the world does not know the love of the Savior.

Sisters, we have been given the gift of the Holy Spirit and His fruit has been planted in us. As we seek the Holy Spirit and turn from the world, the fruit of His love blossoms in us. It grows and matures and we see ourselves being transformed. The way we think about love changes and we start to love like He loves. We can have extreme patience. The victories of others are celebrated and cherished. No longer do we fight to have our own way. Isn't that wonderful? How many of us have sought to be less selfish and more loving? You have been given what you need to thrive!

Let us look at some Scriptures about love and think about how we express love.

What does Ephesians 5:1-2 say about the how and why we walk in love?

1 Corinthians 16:14 tells what things we should do out of love. What are they?

We may feel like living in the Spirit and loving others is hard. Look at 2 Peter 1:2-4. What are all the things we are told we are given in these verses?

How has your definition changed as we looked at this passage? Is it still the same? Why?

Faith Activation: Write a Scripture prayer over Ephesians 5:1-5. A description of how to write Scripture Prayers is provided in the Appendix.

The Holy Spirit is Faithfulness!

If we are faithless, He remains faithful;
He cannot deny Himself.
2 Timothy 2:13

God is the very definition of what it means to be faithful. His faithfulness is all throughout the Scriptures. Faithfulness is the conviction that God is true in all His ways. Our security in Christ is founded on this fact. We can trust that all that He promises will come to pass. As the song "Great Is Thy Faithfulness" says, "There is no shadow of turning with Thee!" Praise Him!

Friend, we are used to how quickly life changes. Things that were true yesterday may not be true today. The people that we thought we could count on abandon us when we need them. Scientific fact that we have taken for granted as true changes and throws our lives into chaos. Look at Pluto, it used to be a planet!

Life has shown me that God, an ultimately Holy Spirit, is reliable and true to His Word. He is a friend at all times! The Holy Spirit is a friend that sticks close to us and does not abandon us when times get hard. The Lord walked the Israelites through the desert as they traveled from Egypt to the Promised Land. He did not abandon them when they built the golden calf or complained.

The book of Psalms talks about His faithfulness in regards to His love for us. It is mentioned in the book 127 times. That is a lot of times. We are told His faithful love endures forever. (Psalm 136) His faithful love towards us is great! (Psalm 117) David says that he will not be removed from the Lord because of His faithful love for him (Psalm 89:33) David was in many battles during his lifetime and he knew who his faithful shield was (Psalm 3:3). God's faithfulness steadies us and keeps us grounded in God!

The times we are living in can feel scary. Fear seems to have gripped a lot of people. A lot of what we have trusted in for so long has crumbled and failed us. God's faithfulness is a foundation that is unshakable. He has delivered us in the past. He will not abandon us now. The rainbow is a reminder that God has kept His faithful promise to never flood the earth again. Dear one, you do not ever have reason to doubt Him.

I mentioned that His faithfulness is our foundation. We need this foundation if we ever hope to walk in the Spirit and experience His fruit to the fullness. That foundation is like the builder from Matthew 7. We build on a foundation that is grounded in His faithfulness and we are stable. The things of life that threaten us cannot tumble us.

The Holy Spirit wants to completely overwhelm you with His faithfulness. Trusting His faithfulness leaves no room for doubt. When we look at His promises in Scripture, we know that they will not change. We can rest in Him because He is always faithful. Thriving becomes possible through letting His faithfulness be the foundation for our lives.

Here are some questions to help you understand how the Holy Spirit is faithfulness!

Let's look at what the following verses say about faithfulness.

Matthew 7:24-27

Psalm 100:5

Psalm 117:2

Hebrews 13:8

In what ways have you seen the Lord be faithful in your life?

Faith Activation: Do a Think on Model about faithfulness. There is a worksheet provided for you.

What Faithfulness Looks Like!

Let us hold on to the confession of our hope
without wavering, for He who promised is faithful.
Hebrews 10:23

It is vital for us to understand the faithfulness of God through the Holy Spirit He has given to us. You do not have to be very old when you learn that not everyone is faithful. We get hurt and scars develop a mistrust of others. Unfortunately, we sometimes transfer this distrust to the Lord. The Holy Spirit wants to shower God's faithfulness in our lives! He wants His faithfulness to carry us through any and every circumstance.

Anxiety has been a companion of sorts in my life, and I will talk about it throughout our study. Overcoming anxiety has taken a lot of mind renewal. Focusing on God's faithfulness calms my heart. One of the things that is helpful is recounting the times when He has been faithful in the past. It reminds me that in the face of what threatens to overwhelm me I am anchored into an unlimited God who will never leave me nor forsake me. This is true for each one of you as well!

God's Word is the best place to start if you want to learn about God's faithfulness. I mentioned the rainbow in the last chapter. God promised Noah that He would never flood the whole world again and each time you see a rainbow, it is His reminder to us, His children.

He promised to be with Israel and his children when they went down to Egypt. He told them to go down to Egypt and after 400 years they would come back to the Promised Land. When they left Egypt all those years later, He promised to go with them. He opened the Red Sea so that they could escape. He promised that they would not be hungry or that their clothes and shoes would not wear out on their journey back. He fed them with manna and their clothes and shoes did not wear out. He was faithful to every promise.

Reading the Word, we see God being faithful to His promises over and over. He promised that if the Israelites would only follow Him, it would go well in their lives. As long as they obeyed the commands of God they prospered. When God sent them into exile with the Assyrians and Babylonians, He promised to bring them back to the Promised Land. Guess what? He did and we see the Israelites rebuilding the wall around Jerusalem in the book of Nehemiah.

One of the most precious promises is that the Lord would provide a way for us to know how to walk with Him. We would not need others teaching us God's ways and showing us how we ought to live. No, He promised a way for us to have a relationship with Him, which He provided through His Son, Jesus. He promised that each man would have within Him all His knowledge and we get that through the Holy Spirit.

Another way to remind us of the faithfulness of the Holy Spirit is to recount His faithfulness in our own lives. In my late 20's it was a great desire of mine to be a mom. It took my husband and I two years to conceive. When I was pregnant with my oldest daughter I was diagnosed with a tubal pregnancy. The ultrasound showed her in my tubes, and they had to schedule surgery. A dear sweet friend told me she would pray for the Lord to move the baby. This baby is now a 22-year-old young woman. He is faithful!

There is power in learning to rest in God's faithfulness. The world wants us to doubt and question what we believe about God. Has He really said that He would never leave us or forsake us? Did He really promise to give you what you need to stand up under temptation? This doubt is an attempt to turn our attention off God and His promises and look at the situation.

It is important to remember that His faithfulness is our foundation for being able to thrive! Spending time remembering the faithfulness of God will equip us to face the future and walk-through times that will try us. It is remembering how He walked us through times in the past keeps us from trying to run, to escape. God has been faithful, and He will be faithful again!

Here are some questions to help you understand even more how the Holy Spirit is faithfulness!

What are some examples of how the Lord has been faithful to you? He loves to hear about the times He walked you through trying times.

I want us to look at more Scriptures about faithfulness. We cannot get enough of seeing His faithfulness!

Philippians 1:6

Hebrews 11:3

Titus 3:5

Exodus 34:6

Faith Activation: Choose one of the verses from the lesson and do a SOAP-F. A description of how to do a SOAP-F is provided in the Appendix.

Love & Faithfulness Working Together!

"Therefore know that the LORD your God,
He is God, the faithful God who keeps covenant
and mercy for a thousand generations with those
who love Him and keep His commandments;
Deuteronomy 7:9

As we start looking at the different aspects of the fruit of the Spirit, it is so important for us to learn of the Spirit. We need to let the Spirit fill us more and more with His fruit. Let Him show you that He is always loving. Let Him show you, His faithfulness. As we learn of and experience the fruit, we renew our minds to what love and faithfulness truly are. In turn, we are conformed more and more into the image of Christ. Then, and only then are we able to mirror these things to the world.

It is obvious that our world has a truly skewed understanding of true love. The Lord wants us to understand what His love truly is and then share it with the world. How can we share that which we do not know? Anything that we share with the world needs to be drawn from walking with the Spirit and letting His fruit well up in us. Let the world see us thrive in His love.

We spent time looking at what love truly is in 1 Corinthians 13. Through getting a taste of what love truly looks like we can mirror it to others. Love does not keep a record of our wrongs. They are all forgiven. Therefore, we do not keep a record of wrongs out of love. We can hope for the best in others. We can be patient and kind towards others. Love is the force motivating all our actions.

Love is what motivates us as we share each aspect of the fruit of the Spirit. It becomes the reason we experience joy, peace, patience, kindness, goodness, faithfulness, gentleness, and self-control. As my mom has said to me often, we can't put the cart before the horse. We start and end all that we do resting in the great love that the Father has lavished on us.

It is not an accident that we are looking at love and faithfulness together. As mentioned previously, we see love and faithfulness together throughout Scripture. Psalm 136 declares the faithfulness of God's love over and over! Let's look at a few of the verses:

Give thanks to the LORD, for He is good;
    For His lovingkindness (graciousness, mercy, compassion) endures forever.

Give thanks to the God of gods,
    For His lovingkindness endures forever.

Give thanks to the Lord of lords,
    For His lovingkindness endures forever.

To Him who alone does great wonders,
    For His lovingkindness endures forever;

To Him who made the heavens with skill,
    For His lovingkindness endures forever;

To Him who stretched out the earth upon the waters,
    For His lovingkindness endures forever;

To Him who made the great lights,
    For His lovingkindness endures forever;

Psalms 136:1-7 (Amplified Version)

This passage says that His lovingkindness endures forever. This is telling us that He is faithful in sharing His love and kindness to us *forever*! He is our greatest example of being faithful. We cannot hope to share His faithfulness towards others until we no longer doubt His faithfulness towards us. We cannot mirror His fruit to others without a right understanding of the Holy

Spirit.

This is an important aspect of thriving in our lives. As we increase and prosper through walking with the Spirit, others will see it. It will attract those who are looking for true and enduring love and faithfulness. We share out of the overflow that is within us. We thrive as we walk with the Spirit!

Here are some questions to help you explore what it means to thrive in love and faithfulness:

How have you seen God express His faithful love to you?

What ways can you share His faithfulness and love to those around you?

Faith Activation: Write Scripture Affirmation about God's faithful love towards you. A description of writing Scripture Affirmations is provided in the Appendix.

Section Three

Joy
&
Peace

The Holy Spirit is Joy!

You will show me the path of life;
In Your presence is fullness of joy;
At Your right hand are pleasures forevermore.
Psalm 16:11

What brings you joy in life? Thinking of joy as things that bring us happiness and contentment images of a lot of things come to mind. Your family can bring you joy. Beauty in nature brings joy. What is truly amazing is the fact that we have a God who is joy and wants to be the source of your joy, not things.

When I started studying joy, it was an elusive concept for me. Joy was just plain hard to describe. It was easy to think of the things that bring joy, but not define it. Wow! Not an easy task. The Greek word for joy in Psalm 16 is śimḥâ. This means happiness, delight, gaiety, pleasurable, and gladness. These are things that the Lord is, and He wants us to find it in Him.

The things that bring joy into our lives, varied as they are, are often perishable. We find joy in a new car, but guess what? That car will eventually get old, break down, and we will need to get a new one. We might find joy in new clothes, but styles change, and the colors may fade. Even people that we find joy in can fail us. These things may bring happiness for a moment.

God wants us to experience Him as joy. The passage in Psalm 16 says that in His presence is fullness of joy. At His right hand are pleasures forevermore. There is no end to His joy when we are with Him. Through the Holy Spirit, who He sends us, we have all of His happiness, pleasure, gladness, and delight always in us. It is not based on what you do or don't do. Joy is there because He is there dwelling in us.

What do we learn from experiencing Him as joy? We see His joy sustaining us when things are not going well. It is a gladness of heart even in the face of trials. His joy never changes depending on circumstances. Sweet friend, we will never face something without His joy, and it strengthens us. "Do not sorrow, for the joy of the LORD is your strength." Nehemiah 8:10

There is no one or no thing that can take the joy of the Holy Spirit from you. Remember, the Holy Spirit dwells inside of each believer in all the fullness of God. The Scripture tells us that there is nothing that can separate us from the love of God in Christ Jesus. The same is true of all the fruit. Looking at joy specifically, isn't that wonderful to know that nothing can separate us from joy? The Holy Spirit wants us to experience the fullness of joy, to thrive in joy!

God's joy is so great. It is big and energizing. The joy we experience is so minuscule compared to the vastness of God's. The feeling of happiness you have from getting a new car, a new job, or even the birth of a child does not compare to what God has for us in His joy. Ephesians 3:20 says, "Now to Him who is able to do exceedingly abundantly above all that we ask or think, according to the power that works in us…" The joy of the Lord is great. Why are we willing to accept so much less?

Living a life in which we thrive, we need joy. It is what nourishes us and flows through us. We see plants growing in places where it seems impossible to grow much less thrive. There is something that is keeping that plant from giving up and letting the heat beat it down. In our lives, there are times when we wonder how we are standing in the face of difficulties. It is His joy coursing through us.

Here are some questions to help you understand the Holy Spirit better!

Think about how you experience joy. What comes to your mind when you think about joy?

In what areas do you think you accept less from the Lord regarding joy?

Faith Activation: Do a Think on Model about joy. There is a worksheet provided for you.

What Joy Looks Like!

"These things I have spoken to you, that
My joy may remain in you, and that
your joy may be full.
John 15:11

I find it so amazing and beautiful that God wants us to experience His joy! He is so full of joy! He is always joy-filled, and He longs for us to be full of joy as well. Jesus told His disciples in the passage above that He wanted the disciples to have joy and that it may be full.

It is worth mentioning that all too often we settle for less than fullness of joy. We settle for mere happiness over true joy. Happiness is based on our circumstances and emotions. Happiness is defined as the agreeable sensation from the possession of something good, an enjoyment of pleasure without pain. There is happiness at being reunited with a long-lost friend. We feel happy when we receive a gift that is exactly what we have desired for a long time. Happiness comes and goes with the changes of life.

The Lord has given me a "Word of the Year" for the last four years. The first time I asked Him for a word, He gave me joy! My youngest daughter was graduating from high school, and I honestly dreaded it. We homeschooled our girls for 11 years and it was hard to think about what it would be like when she started college. When the Lord gave me joy for 2018, I doubted that I would experience any. Honestly, it was a great year. I took two long car trips with my daughter, just her and I, and we laughed and enjoyed being together. She did not go away to college but after dropping her off on her first day, I grieved. When she got home and told me all about her day, I rejoiced. She finally conquered her fear of driving and got her driver's license and again I rejoiced. In a year where I could have really been depressed, the Lord showed me how to find joy in the midst of all that change.

As I write this study, our world is coming out of a year of great turmoil. There has been a global pandemic that has greatly affected our daily lives. We have had many get sick and die. The world's economies have struggled because of this pandemic. The United States has experienced a lot of frustration and hurt over long-term racial injustice. There were peaceful protests and scary riots. There has been so much insecurity in our lives right now and it has felt very scary at times. Many of us have struggled with anxiety. This has not come as a surprise to God. He was not unaware that we would be going through this in 2020. He is still in control and trustworthy. He has not forsaken or abandoned us. He is our source of joy during all this trouble.

There are ways that we, as believers, can cultivate joy in our lives. In the New Testament we see many of the writers encouraging us to rejoice or take delight in our troubles. Look at this passage about joy from James, "My brethren, count it all joy when you fall into various trials,". (James 1:2) This is a theme we see a lot. In fact, many Biblical scholars consider the entire book of Philippians to be discussing joy.

How exactly do we do this? Early in our Galatians passage that we are studying we see the phrase "walk in the Spirit". We have talked about how the Lord wants to have a relationship with Him. We have talked about what walking looks like, sharing our days, thoughts, and emotions with Him. To find joy in the Holy Spirit we need to learn to delight in walking with the Lord. Let's look at the definition:

Delight: to experience a high degree of pleasure and satisfaction of mind; more permanent than pleasure not dependent on sudden excitement.

The Lord wants us to experience a high degree of pleasure and satisfaction in Him. This type of joy is the eternal joy I mentioned in the last chapter.

One of the trials that we can go through is when we are trying to change, and it seems like we struggle repeatedly with the same issue. We work hard to try and change our thoughts and behaviors and end up depressed. When we take delight in walking with the Lord something wonderful happens. Let's look at

Psalm 37:4 "Delight yourself also in the LORD, And He shall give you the desires of your heart."

There is so much in this verse. Taking a close look at it we see that we are encouraged to delight ourselves in the Lord. He wants us to enjoy spending time with Him. He does not want it to be a hardship to spend time with Him. Sing your favorite worship song to Him. Thank Him for His goodness towards you. Tell Him how you are feeling. Enjoy Him!

As you delight in Him, you will find yourself wanting what He wants. You will find yourself thinking like He thinks. The things He shows you will bring a lasting joy to your heart. The things you once desired no longer have power over you. Your anxiety will diminish as you learn of His goodness and love towards you. You will no longer desire control in your life. You will see a desire to fill yourself with food change as you are filled with His joy.

Joy is the part of the fruit that focuses on finding happiness in your relationship with the Lord. As I think about joy, I see it as the part of the Holy Spirit that nourishes my soul. It gives my soul what it needs to stand strong. As a plant draws nourishment from its roots and thrives, so do we as we take in the joy of the Lord!

Here are some questions to help you understand the Holy Spirit better!

Is there an area where you are struggling and would like to experience His joy?

Take a moment to look at Romans 5:3-5. When we rejoice in trials what do we gain?

Faith Activation: Using Roman 5:3-5 write an Scripture Affirmation to help you go through a trail you are facing right now. A description for how to write

Scripture Affirmations is provided in the Appendix.

The Holy Spirit is Peace!

Now may the Lord of peace Himself give you peace always in every way. The Lord be with you all.
2 Thessalonians 3:16

There are so many in our world today seeking peace. We see it in the ways people try to control their lives. They think it's up to them to create peace in their lives. The truth is that we already have peace. We have peace because God is the God of all peace. We have peace because of the indwelling of Jesus who is the Prince of Peace. And we have peace because of the Holy Spirit whose fruit is this peace.

Worry and anxiety plague us today. There are so many different medications, essential oils, relaxation techniques, and mantras to try and keep us in peace. The fact that God is peace and that He has placed His peace inside us through the Holy Spirit should comfort us. We do not need to go looking for it as if somehow, we lost it. It is right there in us.

One of my favorite passages with Jesus is where He and disciples were in a boat and a storm came up. Jesus is asleep in the boat, not even aware of the storm raging around Him. If it had been me, I would have been awake and terrified. The disciples were terrified as well, and they woke Him up to save them. It says in Mark 4:39 that He rebuked the waves and spoke, "Peace, be still." Jesus spoke peace over the storm, and it quieted down. He was able to speak peace because He is peace. I remind myself of this often when I feel afraid!

The Lord wants there to be peace in our lives just as badly as we do. Colossians 3:15 tells us to "let the peace of God rule in your hearts". We do not often put peace and rule together but think about it for a moment. To rule means to govern, to control the will and actions of others. In this case, when we let God's peace govern, control our will and actions, chaos cannot remain. The storm surrounding the boat that held Jesus and His disciples was calmed through Jesus speaking peace over them.

The fruit of the Spirit is the same for God the Father and God the Son. They all three have the same character and produce the same fruit. They just express it in different forms. As someone who has suffered with anxiety for most of my life, I love that one of the characteristics of the Lord is His peace. He wants to share His peace with us. He doesn't just want us to borrow His peace, He wants us to rest in it. He wants us to wrap ourselves up in it. He wants it to affect every area of our lives.

Spending time with Holy Spirit helps us to become so convinced of His great love for us that we are planted firmly on God's foundation. Having our foundation be God's peace will see us through any of life's storms. His peace keeps us from running away at the first trial. Peace helps us to trust the Lord with all our heart so that we do not lean on our own understanding.

Looking at Scripture, we see God's peace all over the place. In the Old Testament we see a blessing of peace in Numbers 6:24-26, "The LORD bless you and keep you; the LORD make His face shine upon you, The LORD lift up His countenance upon you, And give you peace." We see that the Lord is the focus of peace in Isaiah 26:3 "You will keep him in perfect peace, whose mind is stayed on You, because he trusts in You."

In the New Testament we see His peace start with Jesus and it extends to the Holy Spirit. It is the Holy Spirit's work in our lives that produces our peace. "For it pleased the Father that in Him all the fullness should dwell, and by Him to reconcile all things to Himself, by Him, whether things on earth or things in heaven, having made peace through the blood of His cross." Colossians 1:19-20. In the book of Philippians, we see God's peace, which passes all understanding guarding our hearts and minds. God wants His people to rest in His peace.

If we think about what it means to thrive, we have talked about how we flourish and grow and increase. Resting in God's peace is the ultimate place to be in order to thrive. He is like the soil and His peace is the nutrients that feed the roots. Resting in His peace will keep us settled and content and at rest.

Here are some questions to help you understand the Holy Spirit better!

How has God shown you, His peace? How have you experienced it in your life?

Here are some Scriptures to look at as you come to better understand His peace:

John 16:33

John 14:27

1 Peter 5:7

Romans 15:13

Faith Activation: Do a Think on Model about peace. There is a worksheet provided for you.

What Peace Looks Like!

Don't worry about anything, but in everything,
through prayer and petition with thanksgiving,
let your requests be made known to God.
And the peace of God, which surpasses
every thought, will guard your heart
and minds in Christ Jesus.
Philippians 4:6-7

Peace is a gift from God that He gives us through Christ Jesus and the Holy Spirit. There are so many different words that can be used to define peace. It is safety, tranquility, security, or lack of being agitated. We can sit and rest in the wisdom and control of Holy Spirit! This resting is a pause to let Holy Spirit do His work in our lives. As with all the characteristics of the fruit of the Spirit, God is the source of peace.

Peace is often lacking in our lives. While growing up, anxiety was my constant companion. My parents did not have a good marriage. There was a lot of arguing and fighting. Sometimes it would just be verbal arguing and there were times it was physical. As a young child there were many times when I was frightened. There was no one there to talk to about what was happening. Years of being in the environment created anxiety in my life and I was misdiagnosed with epilepsy. Later, I would learn that this was syncope and my body's way of dealing with panic attacks.

My panic attacks continued in my adulthood. It has only been the last couple of years where I have found the true victory that peace brings in my life. There are many different ways that I have seen the Lord deliver me from fear and anxiety. He used His Word. There are so many promises we can lean on to walk in freedom from fear. His faithful and enduring love is a perfect example. Perfect love casts out all fear (1 John 4:18). He brought people into my life to encourage me and point me towards the Lord. Renewing my mind to the truth of who God is has been invaluable.

This passage in Philippians is the perfect example of how His Word has helped me to not be anxious. God's peace acts as a guard, protecting our hearts and minds. This guard depicts an army surrounding a city to protect it from invasion. It keeps the inhabitants of an attacked city from hurting themselves by fleeing an invasion. The peace of God guards our hearts and minds in the same way an army protects. This new understanding is so powerful and freeing. The Lord does not want us to be overtaken by anything and He does not want us to hurt ourselves trying to flee and protect ourselves.

This peace is something that is always at our disposal with the indwelling of the Holy Spirit. The enemy of our soul wants us to stay in a state of fear. The enemy wants us to forget that perfect love casts out fear. There are several tools available to help us renew our minds to the truth of what we have been given by the Holy Spirit. The one that really helped me here is repetition and emphasis. This is repeating this verse over and over, while emphasizing a different word each time. It has helped me to really feel the truth of what peace from the Holy Spirit does for me.

Renewing our minds to the truth that God sends us peace to guard us is comforting. The enemy of our souls does not want us resting in this peace. He wants us trapped under the weight of fear and anxious thoughts. Christ came to set us free from fear and to allow us to thrive.

Here are some questions to help you understand the Holy Spirit better!

What actions can you take to rest in the peace of the Holy Spirit?

Let's look at the following verses and look at what the Word says about peace.

Isaiah 26:3

John 14:27

Psalm 4:8

Faith Activation: Repeat and Emphasize Philippians 4:6-7. A description of how to Relate and Emphasize is provided in the Appendix.

Joy & Peace Working Together!

Now may the God of hope fill you with all joy
and peace in believing, that you may abound
in hope by the power of the Holy Spirit.
Romans 15:13

The fruit of joy and peace are quite a linked pair. They work in a beautiful tandem together. The Apostle Paul asks in the passage from Romans 15:13 that the God of hope will fill us with all joy and peace. Why do they go together so beautifully? Let's take a look.

Joy and peace work together to change our thoughts about a situation. We all struggle in our lives and what we think about is so important to how we will respond. Listening to author and speaker, Graham Cooke, we come to understand how these work together to increase our trust and faith in the Lord.

When we take delight in the Lord, enjoy Him through spending time with Him, our joy increases. The circumstances of life seem less overwhelming. I talked about finding joy even when my daughter was going into a new phase of life where I would be less involved in her day-to-day life. Delighting and finding joy in my walk with the Lord helped me to enjoy that time.

I found that as I delighted in the Lord the Holy Spirit filled me with His peace. Thinking about all that my girls faced when they went off to college, worry seemed to be my constant companion. Have I taught them all then needed to know? Would they remember their manners? Would they make friends? What if they needed me? As I spent time with the Lord and the Holy Spirit filled me with peace, I could trust Him with the girls.

There is this relationship with joy and peace. Joy increases in us as we walk in the Spirit causing us to feel more at peace. As the Holy Spirit's peace floods our soul, our joy increases! A dear friend of mine says that when she is walking in the Spirit and focuses on His ways, she feels like she is spiraling upward, and she is an overcomer. This is why the Holy Spirit shares His fruit with us. He wants us to walk in His power and walk in His freedom.

Looking at the story of Jesus praying in the Garden the night He was arrested; I see Him resting in the joy of the Lord and His peace. He prayed three times for the cup He was about to drink to be removed. He went on to pray that God's will be done. He was facing the Cross and He had to be scared. Hebrews 12:2 tells us this, "…looking unto Jesus, the author and finisher of our faith, who for the joy that was set before Him endured the cross, despising the shame, and has sat down at the right hand of the throne of God." What was the joy set before Him? Reconciling mankind to God. I also see that He was at peace in knowing He was doing God's will. He was able to face the Cross resting in joy and peace.

Here are some questions to help you understand the Holy Spirit better!

How do you see the fruit of joy and peace work to strengthen you in facing trials?

Here are some more verses on joy and peace? What are you learning about joy and peace?

John 16:33

James 1:2

Philippians 4:12

1 Thessalonians 1:6

Jeremiah 15:16

Faith Activation: Today write Scripture Affirmations over the verses we read in today's lesson. A description of how to write Scripture Affirmations is provided in the Appendix.

Section Four

Kindness
&
Goodness

The Holy Spirit is Kindness!

*But when the kindness and the love of God our
Savior toward man appeared, not by works of
righteousness which we have done,
but according to His mercy
He saved us, through the washing of
regeneration and renewing of the Holy Spirit,
Titus 3:4-5*

In the list of the fruit of the Spirit, sometimes kindness falls towards the bottom of the list. We like to think and talk about love, peace, joy, and even self-control. Kindness is just as important as all the other characteristics of the fruit. It is God's kindness towards us that brought us salvation. He knew that you and I could not be holy through our effort. It was kind for God to provide us Jesus to wash us and make us holy.

Kindness is acting in such a way as to contribute and promote the welfare of another person. That is what God has done since the beginning of time. It is evident in the Scriptures how God's kindness is something He wants to show to His people. He wants them to know Him as the God of Kindness and not just the God of Justice. Many times, then, and now we seem to focus on the second one and ignore the first!

In the Old Testament we see His kindness in many of the rich stories. One of my favorites is found in the Book of Ruth. We see Naomi go to Moab with her husband and sons. The sons marry women from that country. Sadly, Naomi's husband and both of her sons die. She decides to return to Israel and her daughter-in-law, Ruth, returns with her. Ruth meets their kinsman, Boaz, and they marry. Ruth has a son and continues Naomi's family line. Also, as an interesting side note, Ruth is included in the genealogy of Jesus. God's kindness is seen through His redeeming of Naomi. He did not forget her and blessed her beyond what she could have asked or imagined.

We see God's kindness in the life of Rahab, the prostitute. It is interesting that almost every time she is mentioned in the Bible it is always noted that she was a prostitute. Rahab hid Israel's spies and helped them escape. She even tells the spies that the reputation of their God has gone before them, and she fears Him. She wants to worship the One true God. Rahab is another woman that God chose to have in the lineage of Jesus. I think it is always mentioned that she was a prostitute to show God's kindness towards her. He did not hold her past sins against her. He saw her faith in Him and chose to write her into His story. Isn't that beautiful?

The ultimate kindness of God is found in the Titus 3:4-5 passage. It was kindness that provided a Savior. It is impossible for us to clean our hearts and minds to the point that we could stand before the Lord! Through sending Jesus, He stepped into history and took on all our sin, nailing it to the Cross. Then out of even more kindness, the Holy Spirit was sent to live in us and regenerate us from the inside out! That is so incredible.

Now that the Holy Spirit is living inside us, we can continually experience His kindness. It is how He desires to interact with each one of us. We can see God's kindness and goodness all around us if we would just look. There have been times when I am backing out of a space and I see another car coming down the lane in time to stop, avoiding an accident! What about when we cannot find something important and after we pray it appears. These are examples of the fruit of the Spirit being poured out over us each and every day! We are able to thrive because the Holy Spirit is kind!

Here are some questions to help you understand the Holy Spirit better!

How have you experienced the kindness of God in your life?

What area of your life would you like to experience some of His kindness?

Let's look at more verses about kindness:

Colossians 3:12

1 John 3:18

1 Peter 3:9

Faith Activation: Do a Think on Model about kindness. There is a worksheet provided for you.

What Kindness Looks Like!

He has shown you, O man, what is good;
And what does the LORD require of you
But to do justly, To love mercy,
And to walk humbly with your God?
Micah 6:8

Does someone specifically come to mind when you hear the word "kindness"? We all have someone in our lives who epitomizes kindness. Everything that they do is kind and thoughtful. They are a pleasure to be around, and everyone has something good to say about them. Our world is so much better for having kind people in it.

Kindness is defined as having the temper or disposition which delight in contributing to the happiness of others. Kindness is done out of love. The Lord is the ultimate example of kindness. He contributed to the happiness of the whole world by sending Jesus to be our Savior. He continues to be kind in providing the Holy Spirit to guide us and remind us of who we are in Christ Jesus. As we walk in the Spirit, His kindness replaces our old ways, and we delight in sharing kindness to others.

I happen to live with someone who is kind. It is my youngest daughter. She is so kind. She loves to help older people at the grocery store. Once we were driving through the store's parking lot during an awful rainstorm. She saw an older lady struggling to put her groceries in her car and battling the rain. My daughter asked me to stop the car so she could help. She grabbed the umbrella and got out of the car. Going over the lady, she held the umbrella over the woman's head. The older lady was able to remain dry. It was so touching to see my daughter care about what was happening to this woman. It was an act of love for someone we may never see again.

We do have examples of kind people around us, but they are not our ultimate example. The kindness that is perfect is the kindness of God. He is always kind. Kindness may not be something you struggle with, but there are times when it is hard. There may be someone you find it hard to be kind towards. This is where renewing the mind becomes so important. It could be that you were hurt by them and want to retaliate. As we meditate on the Word of God, we are reminded that we have the Holy Spirit in us. We can show kindness even when we do not feel like it because of the Helper!

There are times in all our lives where we struggle to be kind to someone. I have a dear friend in my life who shared a secret to being kind to even the most difficult. She would pray and ask the Lord to show her what He loved about that person. He is so faithful and would reveal to my friend what He loved about them. My friend would then be able to pray for that person from a place of kindness. She could understand that person better and would find that it was not so difficult to be kind. The Lord is kind like that!

There are so many different types of kindness. There is the kindness that comes from wanting to share God's kindness with others. Kindness towards others without expecting any reward. Some people are kind just to be kind because it makes them feel good about themselves. As believers the important thing for us to remember is that we need to line our mind up with the truth of God's Word. He has been kind to us because He loves us. Growing out of that love and being motivated by it, we are kind to others.

It is a wonderful blessing to have examples of kind people around us. There are videos on social media of people doing random acts of kindness. People start movements to call for others to do random acts of kindness. How amazing it is to have the ultimate example of kindness in our Heavenly Father! We do not have to imitate anyone in order to be kind. We have the Spirit and His kindness within us causing us to thrive!

Here are some questions to help you understand the Holy Spirit better!

Do you find it hard to be kind? Are there certain people or situations where it is hard to be kind?

How would you like to share kindness with others?

What actions can you take to start renewing your mind about kindness?

Let's look about more Scriptures about kindness:

Luke 6:31

Galatians 5:13

Ephesians 4:32

Faith Activation: Choose one of the verses from the lesson and do a SOAP-F. A description of how to do a SOAP-F study is provided in the Appendix.

The Holy Spirit is Goodness!

Or do you despise the riches of His goodness,
forbearance, and long-suffering,
not knowing that the goodness of God
leads you to repentance?
Romans 2:4

Goodness may seem like it is the same thing as kindness. I know when I first started studying the fruit, I was a bit confused and thought that they were. Goodness, though, is different from kindness because it shows a moral quality. Where kindness is affectionate, caring, generous, and friendly. Goodness is being upright, honest, and having integrity. They can be pictured as two sides of the same coin.

Let's start our study of the goodness of God by looking at Exodus 33:18-20:

Then Moses said, "Please, show me Your glory!" And God said, "I will make all My goodness pass before you, and I will proclaim the Name of the LORD before you; for I will be gracious to whom I will be gracious and will show compassion (lovingkindness) on whom I will show compassion." But He said, "You cannot see My face, for no man shall see Me and live!"

Moses asked to see God's face, but no one can see God's face and live. So, what did God show Him? He showed Moses His goodness. He wanted Moses to be overwhelmed with His goodness. It was important for Moses to experience the goodness of God. That is how the Lord wanted Moses and us to know Him. The Lord could have wanted us to know Him as the God of Justice or the God of Wrath. He wants us to know Him as the God of goodness!

Moses had to veil his face due to being in the presence of God's goodness. This was before Christ came and lives in us now. Where Moses had to hide his face, we get to reflect the glory of God's goodness to the world. We experience

His goodness ourselves, and then share it with others. Moses's glowing face scared those around him. We get to reflect that goodness to those around and draw others towards God.

It is God's goodness that He uses to draw people to Himself. We are living in a period of grace where the Lord is waiting until a full number of people will come to Him for salvation. It is His desire that all would come to Him through Jesus. He knows that not all mankind will do this, but He is waiting as long as possible for as many as possible to put their faith and trust in His Son. It is His goodness that gives Him the patience to wait. His goodness is what draws men to Him, not condemnation or judgment. He longs to overwhelm the world with His goodness, just as He did with Moses.

Dear reader, you may have noticed that I keep using the word overwhelmed in relation to the goodness of God. he God wants us to be overwhelmed every day. I can see how this is true. Each day there are things in my life that seem hard. You know what I mean. We must decide what to do or not to do. The compulsion to react seems to push on us and pull at us. These feelings can threaten to overwhelm us and rob us of all the love, joy, peace, patience…all the fruit. However, by turning to the Lord, we can be overwhelmed by His goodness and all the other parts of the fruit.

The goodness of God is there to strengthen us, to equip us, and to keep us grounded in Him. This overwhelming sense of His goodness causes us to be transformed more and more into His image! The trials of life gives us opportunities to experience more and more of His goodness. Situations that in the past seemed insurmountable shrink! It is His goodness that changes how we view it! His goodness makes us more than over-comers!

When I first started studying the fruit of the Spirit, goodness was hard for me to wrap my head around. The fruit of peace has been easy to understand and explain, but not goodness. So, I asked the Lord to give me a revelation of His goodness. What came to mind instantly was that God provided Jesus for me to have a relationship with Him. He has given me the Holy Spirit so that I can walk in accordance with His will. This alone would be enough but not with our Lord! He wants me (and you) to be overwhelmed by His goodness.

The Lord opened my eyes to how His goodness was with me during some of the darkest times in my life. My family life growing up was difficult. Looking back over these times, I see how God's goodness was there with me. Some of my earliest memories are not good ones. They are colored gray, and I can see the little girl. I was frightened and feeling alone. Yet, the Lord has shown me that He was there with me. Out of His goodness, He was a stronghold for me even as a young child.

Friend, we cannot outrun the goodness of God. "Surely goodness and mercy shall follow me all the days of my life; and I will dwell in the house of the LORD forever." Psalms 23:6 (NKJV) His goodness is always there. We thrive as we get overwhelmed by His goodness and transform into the women He created!

Here are some questions to help you understand the Holy Spirit better!

What do you think of when you think of God's goodness?

How have you experienced His goodness? Ask Him to show you His goodness if you have a hard time seeing it.

Here are some more Scriptures on His goodness:

John 3:15-18

Nahum 1:7

James 1:7

Psalm 84:11

Faith Activation: Do a Think on Model about goodness. There is a worksheet provided for you.

What Goodness Looks Like!

Conduct yourselves honorably among the Gentiles,
so that in a case where they speak against you
as those who do what is evil, they will, by observing
your good works, glorify God on the day of visitation.
2 Peter 2:12

This is probably the hardest characteristic of the fruit to write about. The place we need to start is that God is goodness. Goodness is synonymous with virtuous. They both mean living a morally good life. We can be a person who is morally good and able to be the same person in every situation when we mirror God's goodness.

It would be easy to set up a system of being a good person. We can strive to follow the laws of the land. There are things we can decide that we are just going to do or not do. We will not speed. We will not drink alcohol. We will always tell the truth. The problem we run into here is that we are doing it on our own strength. Paul tells us in Romans 7 that when we want to do good, evil is right there with us. In our own strength we will always fail to be the good person we desire to be.

There is an answer to the dilemma we find ourselves in when we want to do good but find we cannot. It is God. He is good and the Holy Spirit, who is part of the Trinity, has all the goodness of God. We have mentioned before about how as Christians, we have the indwelling of the Holy Spirit. We have the entire fullness of God dwelling in us through the Holy Spirit. That is amazing. When we want to show God's goodness to the world, we need to renew our minds to the fact that we have all we need through the Holy Spirit.

As we renew our minds to this truth, we will see His goodness flow through us to the world around us. We will find a constant in our lives where we are the same person in every situation. People will see that what we believe about God will be lived out in our lives. The verse I opened this study with says that even the lost of this world will see your good works and will glorify God. When we share goodness as an outpouring of our relationship with the Holy Spirit, we glorify God.

Start right now to renew your mind to the fact that we have goodness, that we are good, because of the Holy Spirit. You have the fullness of God therefore we thrive!

Here are some questions to help you understand the Holy Spirit better!

How are you able to share goodness with others?

What steps can you take to renew your mind about goodness in your life?

Look at what the following verses say about goodness.

Galatians 6:10

2 Corinthians 9:8

Ephesians 4:29

Faith Activation: Write Scripture Affirmations using one or more of the verses in today's lesson. A description of how to write Scripture Affirmations is provided in the Appendix.

Kindness & Goodness Working Together!

And we know that all things work together for
good to those who love God, to those who
are the called according to His purpose.
For whom He foreknew, He also predestined
to be conformed to the image of His Son,
that He might be the firstborn among many brethren.
Moreover, whom He predestined, these He also called;
whom He called, these He also justified;
and whom He justified, these He also glorified.
Romans 8:28-30

Kindness and goodness go together so beautifully. Goodness is who God is: He is always just, righteous, honest, and faithful to name a few. Kindness is His action towards us because of His goodness. He shows His compassion because of His goodness. He gives us good things out of His kindness. His kindness is motivated by His goodness.

Goodness and kindness are seen working together in this passage in Romans. God is working everything to our good. His goodness is being birthed in us. He is working in kindness when He does not abandon us in our trials. He takes the trials and uses them to produce in us His character. In Romans 5:3-5 we see Him producing perseverance, good character, and hope. It goes on to remind us that hope does not disappoint us because of His love that He has poured into our hearts through the Holy Spirit. This is the fruit of goodness and kindness at work together.

What is God doing when He provides His kindness and goodness in our lives? He is in the process of conforming us in the image of Christ. It is one thing for Jesus to save us unto eternal salvation, it is bigger and richer for Him to save us in the here and now. His goodness and kindness work in us each day, helping us to put on the things that are in line with the new man. We see the fruit growing up in us and the old things are passing away. We can see the new creation that we are and walk in this creation!

Kindness is His way of showing us His love. We looked at how kindness is His way of offering us salvation. His kindness goes far beyond this. Finding something that was lost for a long time is His kindness towards us. Kindness is not always easy, it cost Jesus His life. Kindness is being loved for who we are and reflecting the love to others. It is choosing to offer help when we lack time and energy. Kindness is being offered a kind word or a smile. Kindness is giving to others without any expectation of return. Kindness is an outward action of how God loves us and how we show that to those around us.

Goodness provides us with a purpose. The world is searching for meaning and purpose. God has not created us to simply exist, but because He has something He wants us to accomplish with our lives. His goodness is poured out over us washing away the things that do not belong to our new nature. Just as Moses reflected the glory of God after seeing His goodness, we reflect that same glory. We reflect His goodness to those around us. This is what gives us purpose and meaning.

God's kindness and goodness work together to see us through trials in life. Romans 8:28-30 says that He causes all things to work for our good. He will take the difficult relationship, the trying child, the need to care for an elderly parent, the struggle to lose weight, or a host of other things and work them to our good. Through kindness, He pours out His love on us. He comforts us with tangible ways that keep us from quitting and giving in. Through goodness, He justifies us and forms us into the image of Jesus.

We are meant to be overwhelmed in this life. For many we are overwhelmed by challenges and frustrations. The Holy Spirit comes in and floods us with kindness and goodness. He overwhelms us with it. We cannot get away from it. It washes us and fills us to overflowing. He wants us to know without a shadow of doubt that He is the giver of good gifts to us as His daughters. His kindness and goodness are what helps us to thrive and grow into women that bring Him glory. Don't be afraid to be overwhelmed by the Holy Spirit. Let

Him show you how great His love is for your through the gifts of kindness and goodness.

Here are some questions to help you understand the Holy Spirit better!

What overwhelms you right now?

How has the Lord overwhelmed you with His kindness and goodness in the past?

Let's look at more Scripture on His kindness and goodness:

Ephesians 3:20

Zephaniah 3:17

1 Peter 4:8

Ephesians 4:29

Faith Activation: Write a Scripture Prayer over one or more of the verses from the lesson. A description of how to write Scripture Prayers is provided in the Appendix.

Section Five

Patience
&
Self Control

The Holy Spirit is Patience!

Now may the God of patience and comfort grant you
to be like-minded toward one another,
according to Christ Jesus,
Romans 15:5

God is patience and we experience His patience through the Holy Spirit whom He sent to dwell in us. That is such an easy sentence to write but it's importance in our lives is so deep. Patience is God's love towards us at it's very best. Walking with the Spirit in His patience helps us to not be moved by the ups and downs of life. In the Spirit, we are able to respond to the things of live and not react to them.

I want us to look at examples from the Word to see how God has been patient throughout history. In the very beginning we see His patience as He confronts Adam and Eve overeating the fruit of knowledge of good and evil. God knew before He went walking in the Garden that Adam and Eve had broken His command. He did not go to the Garden to blast them for their disobedience. He did confront them, but God remained in control of Himself. He told them what the consequences of their actions would be and then He clothed them. He was patient towards them out of His love for them.

We see God's patience over and over as He responded to the Israelites as they journeyed through the wilderness to the Promised Land. They tried Him through complaining about the food He provided. They doubted that He would be able to deliver them out of the hand of Egypt and even considered going back and facing slavery again. When the Israelites built the Golden Calf, God's anger burned towards them, and He threatened to not go with them. Moses pleaded with Him to relent and go with them. God did. He was patient and held back His anger and even gave them victory over some of the nations they traveled through. You and I read this and often say we would not have been as patient. God is patient and He cannot be contrary to His nature. We can praise Him for His enduring patience with us as well!

There is a passage where I see God's patience with an individual. It is in the book of 1 Samuel. We see the prophet Samuel as a young child living in the temple with Eli. In the night Samuel hears someone calling His name and it wakes him. This happens several times and finally Eli realizes that it must be the Lord calling Samuel. God was patient waiting for Samuel and Eli to realize that it was Him calling. God is showing His patience here by not getting angry and overpowering a young boy. He was patient because of His love.

God's patience continues now, this side of the Cross. There are two passages that we will look at in the questions, that talk about how He is long-suffering (patient) because He knows it will lead to repentance. Repentance means to have a changed mind. It is His patience that encourages us to really look at ourselves in light of His truth. For some this inward examination leads to surrendering their lives to the Lord and receiving the ultimate gift of salvation.

Our passage at the beginning of the lesson says He is a God of patience and comfort. Isn't that amazing. Why is patience combined with comfort? It is because He wants to use His patience to comfort us because, as I said earlier, patience is love at its best. It helps us to face the struggles of life. It is a gift to us so that we can stay fixed and immovable as we walk with the Spirit.

For us to thrive we must walk with the Spirit through every situation, good or bad. It is often more difficult to walk through bad or difficult situations. I do not like to feel discomfort. In the past I would have run from hard things. Maybe I would try to numb how I felt so that I did not need to deal with it! When I walk with the Spirit, His fruit develops in my life. His patience becomes my patience.

Think about a time when you were struggling, maybe dealing with an uncomfortable situation. You have two options. First, you could run from it or seek the world for help. We can try to fix whatever is wrong and end up turning to our flesh, the worldly way of dealing with life. Our second option is to turn to the Spirit. We can pour out what we are struggling with and then wait on Him to direct us and work through us. We can rest in His patience. It may take time but that is where renewing our minds come into play. As we wait, we read the Word. We praise Him. This is when we can delight in Him and let His joy strengthen us as we are patient and wait. That is what it looks like to thrive!

Here are some questions to help you understand the Holy Spirit better!

How has God shown you, His patience?

How has the patience of the Holy Spirit helped you walk through different things in your life?

Look at the following verses to get a better understanding of patience.

Psalm 40:1

Psalm 37:7-8

James 1:2-4

Hebrews 6:11-12

Faith Activation: Do a Think on Model about patience. There is a worksheet provided for you.

What Patience Looks Like!

Therefore, God's chosen ones, holy and loved,
put on heartfelt compassion, kindness,
humility, gentleness, and patience,
Colossians 3:12

It is easy to just proclaim we do not have patience and go on our merry way. That is not the truth. In Christ Jesus we have been given the Holy Spirit and He is patient. Everything He has is given to us, this includes patience. Writing this makes me think of my mom. She says that if the Lord had wanted her to have patience, He would have made her a doctor. The truth is, I think she did not want to be patient.

Let's begin by looking at the definition of patience. It is an unruffled temper, or endurance without murmuring. We are told to do everything without murmuring. (Philippians 2:14) Once I was traveling with my small children. We were in the last row of an airplane. As people were starting to deplane, my daughter wanted to push her way ahead. I explained that we needed to be patient and wait our turn. She asked me what being patient meant. The Lord gave me this easy definition for a 3-year-old. Patience means waiting with a good attitude. Do you always wait with a good attitude? No, me neither.

The Lord is a great example of a patient parent. He was patient with His children in the book of Exodus as they grumbled in the wilderness. They did not like the Manna they were given to eat. They were thirsty. In response, the Lord held back His anger and took care of them.

We sometimes think we must strive to be patient with others like He is patient with us. We use so much energy trying to not lose our tempers. We think we must prove to the Lord how patient we can be. Is it any wonder that when we try to be patient and falter, we just give up? We throw our hands up in the air and say, "I can't do it!" The solution to this is to renew our minds to the truth. As we walk in the Spirit, He produces this fruit in us. It is already there for us to rely on. He has already given me all I need for life and godliness. (2 Peter 1:3).

Taking care of my mom can be frustrating. She is slower now and her coordination is off. She cannot follow simple instructions anymore. I find that I just want to fuss at her. It is so hard to wait for her and take care of her with a good attitude. I can leave my times caring for her sad that I have lost my temper with her.

Scripture journaling is helpful with renewing our minds to the fact that we do have patience. The verse I used to be patient with Mom is the one at the beginning of today's lesson. In a journal I wrote out this passage. The truth I see here is that I am God's chosen. I am dearly love. I am holy. As a holy person, I can be compassionate, kind, gentle, and patient. There is no need to beg God to give me patience.

The more we spend time renewing our minds about being patient, the more patience we find we have. He shows me areas where I can be patient with Mom. Instead of getting upset that she wants to take her big mug of water everywhere and worrying she will fall, I offer to carry it for her. The result is a more peaceful time with Mom. We can enjoy doing things together. It is possible to walk away from being with Mom filled with joy and contentment.

Patience is not a part of the fruit that you either have or don't have. Through the Holy Spirit, you have patience. Do not give up if you struggle to be patient. Spend time renewing your mind over this area. Choose verses that tell you the truth of who you are in Christ. You lack nothing and this includes patience. It is helpful to renew before getting into a situation that tests you. We have all the patience we need to thrive.

Here are some questions to help you understand the Holy Spirit better!

Look at the following verses and write out the truths you see about being patient.

Colossians 3:12

Corinthians 13:4

Romans 12:12

Galatians 6:9

Faith Activation: Today as you look at these verses, ask the Holy Spirit to give you a vision about what it looks like to be patient. If it is about a specific situation then ask Him to show you how you can be patient in that area. I would encourage you to write down anything you feel the Lord shows you.

The Holy Spirit is Self Control!

He has not dealt with us according to our sins,
Nor punished us according to our iniquities.
Psalms 103:10

Self-control is a characteristic of God and therefore a characteristic of the Holy Spirit. Due to the unchangingness of God, He is always self-controlled. Look at the passage in Psalm 103. He has not treated us as our sins deserve. It is His self-control that makes Him patient with us, allows Him to speak to us in gentleness, and treat us with kindness. It is the reason that He is the same today, tomorrow, and for all time.

We can look throughout the Scriptures and see examples of His self-control. If we are honest, I think we would all say that mankind has tried God's patience a lot! The story of Noah shows how God regretted making mankind and wiped out all, except for Noah and his family. When the flood waters had receded God placed a rainbow in the sky as a promise to never destroy mankind again. It is His self-control that has kept that promise.

There are so many times in the Old Testament when the Israelites tried the Lord by following other gods. When He called them to be His people, He commanded them to not have any other god before Him. If the Israelites chose to follow other gods, forgetting the One true God, He told them they would be sent into captivity. You may be wondering what this has to do with self-control but wait. He promised to always leave a remnant behind, that He would not completely destroy all His people. Again, this is an example of our God being a God of self-control.

God is such an amazing God! He knows that we will struggle with running headlong into circumstances and situations that threaten to overwhelm us. Looking at the examples of God's self-control, He gives us the Holy Spirit to dwell in us growing the fruit of self-control in us. When we look at our lives, we can see Him using self-control in dealing with us. We see Him speaking to us with gentleness. We see Him being patient with us. He can act out of kindness towards us.

As I have shared, I have struggled with anxiety. Until recently I had not connected self-control with overcoming it. My anxiety usually rears its ugly head when I feel like my life is out of control or there is something I feel is threatening to overtake me. I have experienced a lot of anxiety surrounding my health. What I have come to find out is that when I feel anxiety, that is when the Holy Spirit is there with me. Instead of freaking out I hear the Holy Spirit is gently speaking to me saying, "I have this! Be at peace my daughter!"

I am coming to understand that when I stop and listen to that sweet voice telling me to be calm, it really does help me to calm down. When we remain calm, it is then that we can renew our minds and not react. While renewing our minds we come to see that the Holy Spirit sees so much more of what is going on. His perspective is from the place of eternity. We are able to align our thoughts with His by following this admonition, "*If then you were raised with Christ, seek those things which are above, where Christ is, sitting at the right hand of God. Set your mind on things above, not on things on the earth.*" Colossians 3:1-2

As we will see in our next lesson, self-control can feel heavy. We have all heard the sighs when anyone brings up the topic of self-control. We think that it means we must be strict with ourselves, never having joy in life. That is not at all what the Holy Spirit intends when sharing this part of the fruit with us. My thoughts on self control have changed. It is no longer an obligation. It is a gift and protection! The provision is that we can thrive living a life of moderation.

Here are some questions to help you understand the Holy Spirit better!

What is your experience with self-control?

Have you ever thought about how God shows self-control in dealing with us?

If so, how?

What area would you like to see more of His self-control in your life?

Faith Activation: Do a Think on Model about self control. There is a worksheet provided for you.

What Self Control Looks Like!

For the grace of God has appeared with salvation
for all people, instructing us to deny godlessness
and worldly lusts and to live in a sensible,
righteous, and godly way in the present age,
Titus 2:11-12

Self-control used to scare and frustrate me! It used to be one of those areas that I did not want to try and work on because it seems so unattainable. Thinking about this realistically, it is not so scary. Nor is it as hard as we make it out to be! Stepping back and looking at my life, there are areas where self-control has been easy, like not using swear words. Now, in other areas, it has been more of a struggle. That is fine! Self-control can become a friend to us once we learn what it really means!

Let's look at the definition of self-control. The King James Version uses the word temperance. The definition of the Greek word used in our Galatians passage is the virtue of one who masters his desires and passions. Tapping into the fruit of self control I am able to pursue what is important over what is pressing in screaming for attention. Wow! That puts it into perspective.

Let's look at pursuing the important over the urgent. When we are pursuing the important things in our lives, we are looking to the things of the Spirit. We are desiring the things He desires. His fruit that is in us starts growing into fruit. Personally, I see this happen when I face situations where I need to remain calm and self-controlled. Pursuing the urgent often leads to impulsiveness and uncontrolled behaviors in our lives. We can react out of anger or run to things like food or sex to help cope. It is either turning to the world for help and answers or turning to the Spirit. We already have all that we need in the Spirit so keep turning to Him.

How do we pursue the important and remain controlled? The Titus 2 passage teaches us that we have been given God's grace. It teaches us to say no to our desires and passions that will lead us away from walking in the Spirit. The Holy Spirit then goes on to teach how to live. He teaches us to live a sensible life where we pursue the important things. He teaches us to use the fruit that He has already given us.

We have areas of our lives where we operate from a place of being self-controlled. These may be areas of our lives where we were once impulsive, and the Spirit taught us to be self-controlled. The impulsive behaviors that we do not like may cause us to feel condemnation. That is not where the Lord wants us to live. He forgives, cleanses us, and transforms our thoughts and our actions. One of the tools that helps us change our thoughts is the Think on Model based on Philippians 4:8. As I was studying this area of the fruit the Lord led me to do a Think On Model. The Spirit used this exercise to give me great insight.

Doing a Think on Model brought me to this Titus 2 passage. The truth is that we have the fullness of God through the Holy Spirit. As we walk with the Spirit, He teaches us to use the fruit we have in Him. He teaches us to say no to the things that are not of Him. It is because of Him teaching me to say no to worldly lust that I can say no to Reese's Peanut Butter Cups. He teaches me to say yes to being self-controlled and care for my body.

Not only does self-control help us become more like Christ, but it helps our relationships with others. There are so many different ways I see this playing out in my daily life. The guy that cuts me off while I am driving does not receive my anger. Living in the fruit of self-control, I give him (or her) the benefit of the doubt. I know that I have made mistakes driving. Not getting angry when lines are moving slower than I like or yelling at my husband because he is doing or not doing something I need him to. All these examples come from having an inward focus. The fruit of self-control opens our eyes to others that are around us.

In the last chapter I talked about how self-control is a provision. It truly is a gift from the Spirit for us to keep from finding ourselves in trouble. It helps us to realize the important over the urgent. We are able to live a life of moderation. We can love others in a way that brings glory to the Lord.

Here are some questions to help you understand the Holy Spirit better!

How would you like to see the fruit of self-control in your life

Thinking about how the fruit of the Spirit of self-control is a blessing and provision, has that changed how you think about the aspect of the fruit? If yes, then how so?

Let's look at what the following verses say about self-control.

2 Timothy 1:7

1 Corinthians 10:13

Titus 2:11-12

Faith Activation: Do a SOAP-F over Titus 2:11-12. A description of how to do a SOAP-F study is provided in the Appendix.

Patience & Self Control Working Together!

I, therefore, the prisoner of the Lord, beseech you to walk
worthy of the calling with which you were called,
with all lowliness and gentleness, with long-suffering,
bearing with one another in love, endeavoring
to keep the unity of the Spirit in the bond of peace.
Ephesians 4:1-3

Patience and self-control work so well together. Patience is being calm and unruffled while self-control is making a habit of moderation in one's life. Together they are choosing to pursue the important over the urgent in a persevering manner. These two are gifts to keep us from running headlong into situations and ending up needing to be rescued.

The Apostle Paul talks about walking worthy of the calling of the Lord. I hope by this point that we all know who it is that helps us to walk in a worthy manner and that is the Holy Spirit! The Holy Spirit has been enabling us through the growth of His fruit in us to be gentle, patient, bearing with one another, and keeping unity.

In this study we have been looking at what it means to thrive, to grow, to flourish, and to prosper. When we looked at joy, we talked about how joy is what strengthens us. Patience is the determination to not quit. When we come up against obstacles, and we will come up against them, it is patience that allows us to grow around them. Patience figures out a way to change and adapt to new things in our paths. It is the Holy Spirit working in us to not grow weary in doing well.

In John 15, the Lord Jesus talks about a vineyard and a vine master. The vine master's job is to keep the vine healthy by preparing the soil, clipping away the dead leaves, and keeping the fruit from laying on the ground and rotting. These are not always easy times to grow but they are necessary to become more like Jesus. Patience is needed to stay where the Lord has us and wait on

His growth to develop in our lives. It is often tempting to run ahead and rush or fake growth. Patience is like the trellis that the Holy Spirit uses to help us grow in the direction of the Lord.

Self-control is another example of how the fruit of the Holy Spirit protects us and keeps transforming us into the image of Jesus. Through self-control we can stop and pause in the face of chaos. This pause gives us the ability to talk to the Lord about what is going on. We can come before Him and give Him whatever we feel too overwhelmed to face. We go from reacting to responding. We can proceed and know that we are safe in the arms of Jesus. If patience is the trellis, self-control is the ties used to attach the vine.

Patience and self-control have the same relationship as joy and peace. As our patience increases, we can be more in self-control. And as we can act out of self-control more, our patience increases. The fruit of the Spirit are so interconnected that it gets hard to see distinction between them, and that is the case here.

We do not need to work or practice being patient. We do not need stronger will power to be self-controlled. As I have said before and will say again, this fruit is a gift of the Holy Spirit. He shares His fruit with Him as we walk with Him. We learn what true patience is firsthand. He is patient with us. We see the Holy Spirit acting in self-control. He models it for us. Walking with Him daily changes how we behave.

His patience starts to show itself in how we interact with others and ourselves. We no longer want our own way at the exact time we want it. Waiting is difficult but it produces so many rewards. Remember my daughter asking me what it meant to be patient? She was able to learn and put being patient into practice at an early age. I have seen her walk-in self-control as an adult. She has been in a difficult position since graduating from university. Due to the pandemic, we just went through it has been hard for her to get a professional job. She has worked in an amazing coffee shop but some days she gets so discouraged. Resting in the fruit of the Holy Spirit she can stay where she is and wait for what the Lord will bring to her later!

Through experiencing His self-control, we find ourselves being more in control. No longer do we feel like we have to react. The fear that we will make a wrong choice no longer exists because we are taking the time to look at all sides of an issue from the Lord's perspective and decide on how to proceed. As I have shared before, food is often an area I rush into without thinking. As the Holy Spirit is teaching me what self-control truly is, I find myself making different choices. Recently I was feeling overwhelmed about something and wanted to have chocolate and marshmallows. I went into the kitchen and even opened the chocolate. I felt the Holy Spirit speak gently to my soul. He called me to put it away and look at the situation with Him.

Isn't the Holy Spirit amazing? He is patient and self-controlled and desires for you and me to experience it, personally. We have tried to do these things in our own strength for so long and often end up frustrated. The Holy Spirit is inviting us to walk with Him and learn of Him. He desires for us to thrive through a relationship with Him!

Here are some questions to help you understand the Holy Spirit better!

What relationship do you see between patience and self-control?

What is one thing you can "do" to walk with the Spirit in this area?

Look at more Scriptures about patience and self-control. What do you see in them?

Psalm 37:7-9

Jeremiah 29:11

James 1:19

Colossians 1:11

1 Peter 2:19-23

Faith Activation: Ask the Lord to give you a vision of being patient and self controlled in an area of your life. Be sure to write down what the Lord shows you.

Section Six

Gentleness
&
Delighting

The Holy Spirit is Gentleness!

But the wisdom that is from above is first pure, then
peaceable, gentle, willing to yield,
full of mercy and good fruits,
without partiality and without hypocrisy.
James 3:17

Gentleness is the final fruit we are going to be studying. It is not the least important though. Gentleness is part of the character of the Holy Spirit. He is gentle. He interacts with us out of gentleness. He speaks to us in gentleness. It is beautiful and amazing that we can interact with the God of the universe in a gentle way.

There was a time in my life where I feared the Lord. Not the awesome reverence for the Lord that we are called to have. No, I was afraid that the Lord would strike me. This could be because of how I was raised, or it could be just a distorted view of who God is, but I was afraid of Him. This is not at all how He wants us to think of Him though. He wants to overwhelm us with His gentleness.

Take a moment to remember the moment the Lord spoke to you, calling you to come to Him through salvation through Jesus. For many, I bet we remember the Lord calling to us gently. The church I grew up in always ended each service with an invitation to surrender our lives to Jesus. One of the hymns, *Softly and Tenderly Jesus is Calling*, spoke of God's gentleness. Here is the first verse:

Softly and tenderly, Jesus is calling
  Calling for you and for me
  See on the portals, He's waiting and watching
  Watching for you and for me

Jesus calls to our hearts with softness and tenderness. It is this gentleness that catches our attention because it is opposite of how the world speaks to us.

Gentleness does not stop working in us once we come to Jesus. In Matthew 11 verses 28 & 29 we read: "Come to Me, all you who labor and are heavy laden, and I will give you rest. Take My yoke upon you and learn from Me, for I am gentle and lowly in heart, and you will find rest for your souls." He wants us to experience His gentleness right now.

The process of becoming more Christ-like can be challenging. As we walk in the Spirit, we are taking off the old man, laying aside our earthly ways of dealing with life. We are putting on the new man, the man that is created in Christ's image, created with good work for us to do, and created to walk in the fullness of God. This process, called sanctification, can feel hard but when we take up Jesus's yoke, we experience His gentleness wash over us. We feel His love for us, and we feel His power spurring us on to the good works He has prepared for us.

The gentleness of the Holy Spirit is experienced in how He talks to us. There is a picture on my wall of Jesus holding a lamb in His arms. You know it is Jesus because of the nail scar in His hand. You cannot see His face because He is whispering in the lamb's ear. The lamb has such a look of contentment and peace. This is how the Holy Spirit speaks to us now. Through His gentleness we experience contentment and peace.

This image of Jesus being the good shepherd is probably familiar to you. I love what it says in Isaiah 40:11, "He will feed His flock like a shepherd; He will gather the lambs with His arm, and carry them in His bosom, and gently lead those who are with young." His desire is to be gentle with us. He loves us and this love motivates His actions towards us. His gentleness allows us to rest in Him and to thrive.

Here are some questions to help you understand the Holy Spirit better!

Do you see the Lord as gentle? Why or why not?

Look for a story in the Bible that shows the Lord's gentleness and share it here.

Let's look at more Scriptures about His gentleness:

2 Samuel 22:36

Psalm 23

Isaiah 42:2-3

Psalm 45:4

Faith Activation: Do a Think on Model about gentleness. There is a worksheet provided for you.

What Gentleness Looks Like!

"Therefore I, the prisoner for the Lord, urge you to walk worthy of the calling you have received, with all humility and gentleness, with patience, accepting one another in love, diligently keeping the unity of the Spirit with the peace that binds us."
Ephesians 4:1

God is gentle with us. He does not treat us as our sins deserve. He gave His mercy. His gentleness is seen in His patience with the world in order that as many people will come to Him as possible. He is tender in picking us up when we fall. He forgives us our sins and cleanses us from all unrighteousness. (1 John 1:9) He comforts us when we are broken hearted. In His gentleness He is humble.

Gentleness is not self-absorbed or having a feeling of superiority. Just as important it is not feeling inferior to other. Jesus is the perfect example as seen in Philippians 2:5-8. In this passage we see a perfect example of humility not being the same as inferiority. Jesus is God but He lived as a simple carpenter. He willingly went to the Cross so that we could be reconciled to God for all eternity.

When we look at Jesus as our example of gentleness, it would be easy to give up and think that we cannot even come close to Him. That is not true. Remember, we have been given the Holy Spirit. The fullness of God dwells in us through the Holy Spirit. His fruit is in us and is available at all times. This is what we need to renew our minds over. We do not need to beg for His gentleness. As we look at what the Word says about His gentleness, it is birthed in us and grows.

My emotions can be rather strong, and anger was a huge struggle when I was younger. Anger seems to be the opposite of gentleness in some ways. Anger is a reaction to not getting my own way. It is having to put my desires to the side in favor of someone else. Getting married, having children, and caring for Mom made it impossible for me to ignore my struggles with anger. It came out in the tone of voice. It was visible as I would stomp around or open and close cupboards more loudly than necessary. Anger seemed to rule me, and gentleness went out the window!

Last year I took the course Renewing the Mind 101, by Sophia Tucker. In it there are tools on how to renew the mind. They are the ones I am using here. One of the mind renewal tools is using our imagination. It is asking the Holy Spirit to give a picture (an imagining) of what walking in Him looks like in a certain situation. Taking care of my mom has really tested me and I asked the Holy Spirit what being gentle towards my mom would look like. He was so faithful and gave me a vision of what this practically looks like.

The image He gave me was very similar to caring for my girls when they were young. It was a vision of helping Mom bathe herself. It is making sure she is not alone so she will not hurt herself. It was a vision of her wrapped in a towel, smiling at me as I helped her dry off. The vision grew to where I was tucking her in at night. I saw myself making sure she had enough blankets and saying bedtime prayers with her. It was holding her hand as she cried over all the awful changes that were going on around her that she felt threatened to overtake and destroy her.

This vision was so strong and clear. Each day, before interacting with Mom I would pray and review the vision He gave me. I would imagine myself acting in gentle ways with her. On the days I did this, there would be such peaceful times with Mom. She would be happy, and I could rest in the knowledge that I was gentle towards her.

It is something I had never tried before. After renewing my mind this way, I find it is easier to walk in the Spirit. Looking at the situation only brought heartache. Everything within me wanted to change the situation and make her not have dementia. It was a fight. Looking at the Holy Spirit I saw His gentleness. His gentleness flowed through me to my mom. Focusing on the

Spirit, gentleness blossoms and we thrive!

Here are some questions to help you understand the Holy Spirit better!

How have you experienced gentleness in your life? Either from the Lord or others in your life?

What actions can you take to renew your mind about gentleness?

Let's look at what the following verses say about gentleness.

Titus 3:2

2 Timothy 2:24-26

James 3:17

Faith Activation: Choose one of the verses for the lesson and write a Scripture Affirmation. A description of how to write Scripture Affirmations is provided in the Appendix.

Abide in the Spirit!

"I am the vine, you are the branches. He who abides
in Me, and I in him, bears much fruit;
for without Me you can do nothing.
John 15:5

We started out our journey together talking about the importance of walking with the Spirit. We learned that when we walk with the Spirit, we carry out the desires of the Spirit. Walking in the Spirit is how His fruit develops in our lives. Walking with the Spirit is the same as abiding in Jesus. Our focus is on Jesus and the Spirit, relying on them over ourselves.

Abiding in Jesus is to exist, continue, remain, dwell, or to remain stationary. This is a state of relying on Jesus versus relying on the self. Jesus is producing fruit in us because He is the vine. The vine feeds the branches and prepares the branch to bear more fruit and in abundance. On its own a branch cannot bear *ANY* fruit. Jesus was talking to His disciples in this passage. They were able to hear His teaching and watch how He lived. Today we have been given the Holy Spirit to remind us of Jesus' teaching. We are abiding then as we walk in the Spirit, dwelling and remaining close by His side.

The Holy Spirit wants to overwhelm us with the fruit. This is a desire we have seen throughout this study. He wants to overwhelm you with love. He wants to overwhelm you with peace to calm anxiety causing chaos to lose its control over you. How can we become so overwhelmed with the fruit unless we are abiding in Him? Thinking of the vine analogy, if we are not attached to the Spirit, not abiding in Him, then this will not be true in our lives. We will find ourselves being tossed by every wave and feeling utterly drained.

What does this look like practically? There is a choice we make with every situation we face. When we turn to the fruit of the Spirit instead of turning to the works of the flesh, we find patience. We can be in control of our temper. Turning to the Spirit overeating to numb our feelings we find self-control. This may look like us stopping and taking a step back. Praying and asking the Lord to reveal what is going on in a situation. The faith actions we have done throughout this study are tools to turn to in order to renew our minds. Believe me, the more we find ourselves turning to the Spirit instead of ourselves, the more we will see the evidence of the fruit in our lives. As we abide, we thrive.

Here are some questions to help you understand the Holy Spirit better!

In your life, what would it look like for you to abide in the Holy Spirit?

What are some steps that you can take today to develop a lifestyle of abiding?

Let's look at some Scriptures to give us more insight into abiding:

1 John 2:27

2 John 1:19

Colossians 1:27

Faith Activation: Repeat & Emphasize John 15:5. A description of how to Repeat and Emphasize is provided in the Appendix.

Delight in the Lord!

Delight yourself also in the LORD,
And He shall give you the desires of your heart.
Psalms 37:4

I have so enjoyed our journey with the Holy Spirit! His fruit is wonderful, and it is through experiencing the fruit we see how we can thrive! It is my prayer that you have learned something new through this study. Maybe you have learned something new about the Holy Spirit. There is such depth to Him. In studying Him and the fruit, I see how much I did not know about Him. My understanding of Him has grown from thinking His main job was to convict me of my sin. Now I see that He has such wonderful and great gifts for me!

This study has gone through the different aspects of the fruit pretty quickly, but the journey is not over! There is still so much to learn about the fruit. In fact, I would guess that this is a journey we are only just beginning. Where do we go from here? How do we keep up the momentum that we started?

When we began, we looked at walking in the Spirit. We did that little exercise about imagining walking with a friend. I hope that you are now able to see the Holy Spirit as your friend. The truth is, in Christ, He is always your friend. What keeps you walking with a friend for the long haul? You enjoy being in their presence! That is what we are going to look at today as we finish out our study.

This passage in Psalm 37 has truly become a favorite of mine! It is a verse I am drawn back to often. What does it mean to delight? Delighting means to take great pleasure in something or someone! Looking deeper, to delight means to have satisfaction and experience joy. This is how the Lord wants us to experience Him. As we walk with Him, He wants us to enjoy being with Him, to find our satisfaction and joy in Him.

The fruit of the Spirit are not to be a list of things we must "do". They are meant to be experienced as we face every day with the Spirit. The Spirit wants to overwhelm you with His fruit. He desires us to be delighted by His love for us. He wants to have His peace fill us to overflowing. The fruit is the activity of the Spirit working in our lives.

Practically, what does it look like to delight in the Lord? How do we do it? As with walking with the Spirit, we delight by being in His presence. We delight when we worship Him, telling of His wonders. Being with the Lord does not need to be drudgery. It can be a time of fellowship. Talk to Him about anything and everything.

It is possible to delight in Him by reading His Word. You come to know His thoughts and desires through His Word. He has a sense of humor that comes through in the Word. The things that touch His heart, that are important to Him come out as you read and meditate on the Word. He encourages us to taste and see that He is good. Let's look at Psalm 119:103-104

How sweet are Your words to my taste,
  Sweeter than honey to my mouth!
  Through Your precepts I get understanding;
  Therefore I hate every false way.

It is possible to thrive when we walk in the Spirit, delighting in Him. The fruit of the Spirit is a gift to us to enjoy Him. We experience this delight through spending time with Him. Situations in our lives can threaten to overwhelm us. We face a choice with these situations. We can choose to be overwhelmed by the bigness of what we face. Our flesh, the un-renewed part of us, will rise up and try to fix whatever is going on. Through experiencing the fruit, we have another option.

We looked at peace and how anxiety threatens to steal it away. As I said, we could try to fix it or make it go away in our own power. The other option is to turn to the Spirit. Look to Him as our source of strength to go through whatever threatens us. Through prayer and or reading His Word we can turn the situation over to Him. We can let His peace overwhelm us and keep our hearts and minds guarded.

We have looked at the definition of thriving many times during our study and it means to flourish, to grow, and to prosper. The fruit of the Spirit is provision that the Lord gives us. It is like the water that flows over us and through us. It washes us clean. It wells up inside us creating beauty and vibrancy. Let's delight in the Lord and thrive!

Here are some questions to help you understand the Holy Spirit better!

What comes to your mind when you think of delighting in the Lord?

What keeps you from delighting in the Lord?

What can you do today to start taking delight in the Holy Spirit?

Let's look at some Scriptures about delighting in the Lord:

Psalm 119:33-40

Zephaniah 3:17

Jeremiah 31:3

Deuteronomy 33:27

Faith Activation: Choose one of the verses from the lesson and write out a Scripture Prayer about delighting in the Lord. A description of how to write Scripture Prayers is provided in the Appendix.

Study Review

This is the end of our study. We have covered a lot of ground and today I want to give you space to review what you have learned. Looking at the following areas, what is something you learned?

- The Holy Spirit

- Love

- Joy

- Peace

- Patience

- Kindness

- Goodness

- Faithfulness

- Gentleness

- Self-Control

- Abiding in Love

- Delighting in the Lord

What is one overarching message you received during our journey with the fruit of the Spirit?

Which faith activation do you find most helpful and why?

I want to thank you for taking this journey with me. It has been amazing to look at each of the fruit. We have been able to renew our minds about what we have in Christ. Hopefully you have a greater understanding of how the Holy Spirit wants to overwhelm you with His fruit. We experience it as we walk with Him through our daily lives. There is no end to what He wants to grow and develop in us. The Holy Spirit wants us to Thrive!

Appendix

Scripture Cards - This is simply writing Scripture on index cards to carry with you and have handy and ready. Pray and recite them throughout the day.

Affirmations - These are just making the Scriptures personal. We add our names or "I" and even insert specific situations. "I seek love when I cover transgressions, but if I chose to repeat a matter I can separate friends." Proverbs 17:9

Scripture Prayers - Turn a Scripture into a personal prayer. "Lord, let me first show godliness to my own household and my parents. I desire to please you in honoring and serving them with Your love." 1 Timothy 5:4

Repeat and Emphasize: We take a Scripture and break it up into words or sections and repeat the Scripture over again emphasizing each word or section in sequence. Here is an example: "**Give** thanks to the Lord!" "Give **thanks** to the Lord!" "Give thanks **to** the Lord!" "Give thanks to **the** Lord!" "Give thanks to the **Lord**!"

SOAP-F Study -

S - Scripture: Write down the Bible passage you will be studying. This can be one verse or several. I have found that writing the verse out helps me focus on each word individually and on the passage as a whole. It also helps me soak it in and meditate on it.

O - Observation: Examine the text and write down what you notice in the passage. What jumps out to you in the passage? Who is it written by? Who is it written to? What's one thing you have not noticed before? What seems interesting or unusual? What comes before and after the text? Is there repetition, comparison, or contrast?

A - Application: Apply God's Word to your life n a practical way. This is the part where you personalize your study of Scripture. As you read over the text, how does it apply to you? Is there a specific action you need to take or a confess you need to make?

P - Prayer: Respond to God's Word with your own words. Accumulating head knowledge about God is of little use; it's heart transformation He is after, and that is only possible through the work of the Holy Spirit.

F - Faith Action: Externalize your area of faith you are believing God for with a suitable action. For example with the guidance of the Holy Spirit, consider how can you be a doer fo this Word? What actions can you take to renew your mind today? Affirmations? Scripture Prayers? Etc. Then, do these outwardly in order to consolidate the renewing the mind process several times a day or over the week.

This was taken from the blog www.onethingalone.com.

The F - Faith Action was taken form the SOAP-F section of the blog www.sophiatucker.com.

Made in the USA
Las Vegas, NV
24 August 2021